The Introvert Ent

D1104150

"Filled with powerful stories from entrepreneurs in all stages of business, along with actionable advice, this book is an essential resource for introverts who choose to follow their entrepreneurial vision and carve out their own unique path."

—Susan Cain, cofounder of Quiet Revolution LLC and *New York Times* bestselling author of *Quiet: The Power of Introverts in a World That Can't Stop Talking*

"As a longtime introvert entrepreneur, I was thrilled to discover a toolkit of resources for others like me. This book shows how you can go your own way while still being true to yourself. You can be successful in business without shouting—and you don't have to attend those boring 'networking' events either."

—Chris Guillebeau, *New York Times* bestselling author of *The $100 Startup* and *The Happiness of Pursuit*

"I have always loved listening to Beth Buelow's engaging podcasts. What a treat it is for all of us to learn from her in this well-written and practical book. If you think only extroverts can sell or lead thriving businesses, you will change your mind after reading *The Introvert Entrepreneur*. Interested in joining the growing ranks of entrepreneurs? This book is the definitive guide to have at your side."

—Jennifer B. Kahnweiler, PhD, author of *Quiet Influence*, *The Introverted Leader*, and *The Genius of Opposites*

"Having followed Beth's work and then reading *The Introvert Entrepreneur*, I've realized that many of my ways of engaging with introverts were always based on my preferences rather than considering theirs. Now armed with increased understanding, I've changed my style and am getting better results in my communications with them. This book now has a permanent home on my desk as a valuable reference."

—Christopher Flett, founder of Ghost CEO and author of *What Men Don't Tell Women About Business* and *Market Shark*

continued . . .

"As an introvert, entrepreneur, and salesperson, I have been waiting for a book like this one. I just didn't know it. Beth Buelow provides the essential guidance and encouragement for those labeled as introverts with the passion to grow their businesses."

—John E. Doerr, co-president of RAIN Group and author of
Insight Selling: Surprising Research on What Sales Winners Do Differently

"Beth Buelow's gem of a book is a coach and mentor in your pocket that celebrates your strengths, facilitates your creative thinking, and cheers you along (quietly!), step by step, toward your entrepreneurial dreams. Buelow spurs you to unleash the best of what you have to offer—from reflection to action, from your FUD (fear, uncertainty, doubt) to your prosperity perspective."

—Nancy Ancowitz, author of *Self-Promotion for Introverts*

"Finally, a book about entrepreneurship that celebrates the gifts, skills, and strengths of introverted business owners. The stories, tools, and frameworks will guide and support effective, sustainable business growth for introverts in every type of business."

—Pamela Slim, author of *Body of Work* and *Escape from Cubicle Nation*

"In this book, Beth takes you on a powerful journey, dismantling each of the destructive limiting beliefs that most of us introverts have about why we can't be successful entrepreneurs. This book is an empowering triumph for quiet leaders."

—Rory Vaden, *New York Times* bestselling author of *Take the Stairs*
and *Procrastinate on Purpose*

"What introverted dreamer wouldn't want a smart, successful mentor available in the quiet of their living room? Beth Buelow is just that, and *The Introvert Entrepreneur* reaches introverts where they live: inside, with their hopes, fears, and questions. An indispensable guide."

—Laurie Helgoe, PhD, author of *Introvert Power:
Why Your Inner Life Is Your Hidden Strength*

"With wisdom and compassion, Buelow teaches introverts not just how to survive the rigors of entrepreneurship but how their particular gifts and quiet strength can help them thrive and prosper."

—Sophia Dembling, author of *The Introvert's Way* and *Introverts in Love*

The Introvert

Entrepreneur

AMPLIFY
YOUR STRENGTHS
AND CREATE SUCCESS ON
YOUR OWN TERMS IN TEN STEPS

Beth Buelow

1 3 5 7 9 10 8 6 4 2

Virgin Books, an imprint of Ebury Publishing,
20 Vauxhall Bridge Road,
London SW1V 2SA

Virgin Books is part of the Penguin Random House group of companies
whose addresses can be found at global.penguinrandomhouse.com

Penguin
Random House
UK

First published in the United States by Perigee in 2015
First published in the United Kingdom by Virgin Books in 2015

www.eburypublishing.co.uk
A CIP catalogue record for this book is available from the British Library

ISBN: 9780753556832

Printed and bound in Great Britain by Clays Ltd, St Ives plc

MIX
Paper from
responsible sources
FSC® C018179

Penguin Random House is committed to a sustainable
future for our business, our readers and our planet.
This book is made from Forest Stewardship Council®
certified paper.

Contents

CONTENTS

You are a walking contradiction.

On the one hand, you are an introvert. You tend to prefer ample alone time. You appreciate blocks of uninterrupted time so you can focus. You enjoy going deep rather than broad in whatever catches your fancy.

On the other hand, you are an entrepreneur. You are required to interact with employees, partners, clients, and customers on a regular basis. You must be accessible and responsive, even when it's not convenient. You have to wear multiple hats, taking on everything from product development to social media to finances.

How can one person be both of these things and remain sane? This book is an attempt to answer that question as well as give you, the introvert entrepreneur, tools not only to save your sanity but to build a business that feeds your soul.

Since 2010, I've been coaching introvert entrepreneurs—those who own their own businesses and those who are "intrapreneurs," assuming an entrepreneurial role within a larger company—and there are certain challenges that come up over and over again. Here's how my clients typically describe those challenges:

Networking: It's exhausting. People are just trying to sell to each other. It's full of small talk, schmoozing, and insincere invitations to get together sometime.

Sales: I'm not very good at it. I dread making calls. People will think I'm bothering them. The phrase *sales funnel* makes me want to run for the hills.

Self-promotion: It's challenging to talk about what I do without tripping over my words. I'm hesitant to toot my own horn; I don't want to come across as bragging or arrogant.

Collaboration: I tend to wait until the last possible minute to ask for help. It's a lot of work, bringing other people into my business and bringing them up to speed. And if I do start a partnership, I'm concerned our personalities will clash.

Energy: I'm supposed to be out and about so much, but it wears me out. I need lots of downtime so that I have the energy to network and market my business. There don't seem to be enough hours in the day for it all.

These entrepreneurs are not complaining or whining. They are simply noticing the areas that drain their energy and stall their progress. And while these challenges aren't unique to introverts, how introverts experience and navigate these challenges *is* unique. We work from the inside out. We internalize, analyze, and sometimes even become paralyzed by the energetic tug-of-war that goes on between our private introvert nature and our public entrepreneurial passion.

> *I have the fire, the drive, the know-how. But I've been in the shadow of extroverts for so long, it's vulnerable to step out of the shadows and into the light.*
> —Helen Sanderson, owner, Quiet Room Designs

The Introvert Entrepreneur: Amplify Your Strengths and Create Success on Your Own Terms in Ten Steps does what no other book on introversion or entrepreneurship has done: It explores a range of entrepreneurial topics from an introvert point of view, including how your personality and energetic type play a role in building a sustainable business; fears, mindset, failure, and self-management; values identification; networking, marketing, and sales; creating community; and partnership and expansion.

The Introvert Entrepreneur directly takes on the mistaken but prevailing assumption that entrepreneurial success belongs to the extroverts. This book shares the stories and lessons from introverts who have chosen to defy that assumption, built successful businesses, and created a way of life that honors their natural energy. Rather than seeing introversion as a liability (as most of society treats it), this book provides a road map for entrepreneurs who want to cultivate and amplify their natural, internal strengths.

What many people, including introverts themselves, may not know is that the strengths and traits of the typical introvert—curiosity, desire for depth over breadth, comfort with going solo, thoroughness and introspection, love of research—lend themselves well to entrepreneurship.

Introvert entrepreneurs such as Bill Gates, Larry Page, Mark Zuckerberg, Jeff Bezos, Tony Hsieh, Guy Kawasaki, and others have transformed our lives not by pretending to be extroverts but by applying their introvert strengths to their entrepreneurial endeavors.

An introvert trying to be a fake extrovert is just that: a fake extrovert. If you choose to approach your business with that mindset, you won't solve your problem. You'll only feed the energetic tug-of-war between your private and public personas.

The Introvert Entrepreneur acknowledges the particular road-blocks you may encounter when building a business. But it also takes a strengths-based approach to being a successful entrepreneur. Your introversion is a tremendous asset in ways that might not be obvious in our extrovert-leaning world. For instance, you may see yourself in several of these positive traits:

- Ability to focus and develop a depth of understanding
- Comfort with independent thought and action
- Capacity to listen and connect with people on an intimate level
- Active imagination and a strong creative streak
- Desire for knowledge, driven by curiosity
- Calm, steady presence during turbulent times
- Willingness to put other people and their vision in the spotlight

You may have read one of the many books that provides general information about the nuts and bolts of entrepreneurship. This book, however, focuses more on your *relationship* to the nuts and bolts, which is a critical link. It addresses the oft-heard lament: "I know what to do, so *why don't I do it*?"

We can be motivated and excited, but fail to execute on our passions. *Successful execution for the introvert depends on being in alignment with one's energy and strengths.*

One of the reasons introverts choose entrepreneurship is so that they can live and work authentically, according to *their* rules . . . yet, so many of the rules are created by extroverts. Learning how to build a sustainable business that emphasizes authenticity, personal and professional relationships, and energy management while leveraging introvert strengths is difficult when much of the available information is provided from an extrovert framework.

This book aims to fill that information gap.

We're not going to dive deep into research or statistics; there are plenty of other resources that do an excellent job going into the mechanics of introversion or entrepreneurship. Instead, we're going to rely on practical advice, personal experiences, and lessons learned from introvert entrepreneurs at every stage of their journey. We'll dissect the fears, challenges, and opportunities that we encounter every single day.

I invite you to see this book as your personal coach, mentor, and reality check. It's part cheerleader, part gentle push off the cliff. Meditate on each chapter or read the book all in one sitting. Make the most of the book's online resources. Reach out to the people who offered their wisdom to you through this book. And, as with any advice you receive about living as an introvert or building your business, some of what you read here will resonate and some of it won't. Take what works and leave what doesn't.

With every growth opportunity, you get out of it what you put into it. I've poured the best of my heart and mind into this book, and I invite you to do the same.

Chapter 1

Introversion 101

What Does It Mean to Be an Introvert and an Entrepreneur?

The Perception

One evening a few years ago, I attended an event sponsored by my professional coaching association. I was seated next to a colleague and his wife, and we were exchanging pleasantries about the event and people we knew. Then the conversation inevitably turned to our work. My colleague's wife shared that she was a schoolteacher and asked me if I was a coach like her husband. I told her, "I am, and I specialize in working with introverts." She was very curious about what that meant, so I explained to her why introverts have a particular set of opportunities and challenges when operating in a more extroverted society. She listened politely, then asked, "Well, are *you* an introvert?" I replied, "Most definitely!" She was flabbergasted. "But you can't be an introvert! You're talking to me!"

Has something like that ever happened to you? Did you know that according to the media and maybe even your friends and family, if you're an introvert, you're probably shy, a poor conversationalist, a loner, depressed, without many friends, a geek, or even a serial killer in waiting? All of these misunderstandings and more are part of the general myth of what it means to be an introvert. While we've made progress in recent years, there's still an excess of negative stereotypes that are attached to the label *introvert*. The assumptions people make about introverted types range from the benign shy to the more harmful sinister.

We are in the midst of a sea change, in which introversion is being more widely understood and accepted. We have long lived in the shadows, challenged by stereotypes that have seeds of truth but are inaccurately applied to the whole. As author and activist Jonathan Rauch remarks, "In all of these consciousness-raising movements, the first step is embracing the stereotype. But then the second step is moving beyond the stereotype."

In the spirit of leaving those less-than-flattering perceptions behind and moving beyond the stereotypes as quickly as possible, let's take a closer look at what it really means to be an introvert.

The Reality

Understanding the true definition of *introvert* can be extraordinarily empowering and liberating. And yet, because introversion is still not well understood by most people, we can find ourselves defending our choices or disowning what comes naturally to us. Even those who love us can think we need to be fixed in some way. They encourage us to get out of our shell and tell us not to be afraid to speak up. We decide they might have a point, even as we think to ourselves, "Maybe I like my shell" and "I'm not afraid, I just don't have anything to say at this point." We start doubting ourselves and our social skills, and "Fake it till you make it" becomes our mantra for everything from birthday parties to networking events.

The reality is that introversion inherently has nothing to do with social skills and everything to do with how a person gains or drains energy, processes information, and relates to the world.

If introvert entrepreneurs are to step into their power and claim the strengths inherent in their personality, it's important to be clear on what it means to be an introvert. Swiss psychologist and psychiatrist Carl Jung coined the terms *introvert* and *extrovert* in the early 1920s.[1] Jung was initially a student of Sigmund Freud in the 1910s. The two had a falling-out, and Jung was fascinated by the different ways each of them had of relating to the world and communicating their ideas. This led Jung on a quest to identify the root causes of their differences, which he found to be related to their orientation to the world, Jung's being inward, and Freud's outward. According to the Jung lexicon, *introversion* is "a mode of psychological orientation where the movement of energy is toward the inner world."[2]

While that's the original formal definition, introverts have their own way of describing their personality. When I conducted a survey of introverted business owners, they shared these insights about how they defined *introvert*:

We are drained after lots of social interaction. "I was taught in college that an introvert is a person who finds interacting with people to be tiring and an extrovert gets energy from interacting with other people. I had a hard time believing that there were actually people who would come home from a particularly difficult day at work and would want to go out to a party or to see people in order to feel better. I still have a hard time believing it."

We sometimes exert more energy on not being seen than it would take to be seen. "During school I worked harder at *not* speaking in front of my classmates than if I had just done it. Took many F grades to not be up in front of the class and would rather write huge reports instead."

We process internally. "Someone who is introspective, who has excellent reflection skills, who in actuality has excellent communication skills because he is generally a fantastic listener. Overall, pretty awesome."

We enjoy being alone. "Someone who is self-contained and can enjoy activities by themselves."

We need our alone time. "A person who requires alone time to recharge his or her batteries."

We're focused on ourselves. "Introversion is a preference of being in my thoughts and feelings more than around other people and theirs. By honoring this, I bring my best energy and enjoy being with others for conversation and friendship."

As one of my friends puts it, an introvert can be "happy as pie" spending time alone. An extrovert is likely to become restless or lonely after fifteen minutes of solitude, especially if that solitude's not been balanced out by a healthy dose of energizing social interaction.

In addition to Jung's theory, there is research from the 1960s conducted by German psychologist Hans Eysenck that provides a biological basis for the definitions of *introversion* and *extroversion*.[3] Eysenck found that responses to stimuli varied between introverts and extroverts. Introverts had naturally high cortical arousal, which means they reached their stimulation saturation point much more quickly than did extroverts.[4] This explains why large social gatherings or noisy environments can be stressful for introverts. It seems to be a complement to the Jung theory of energy: It makes sense that introverts would drain energy in high-stimulation environments because our circuits become overloaded. To replenish our reserves, we need to limit the amount of external input coming our way.

Throughout this book, our discussion of introversion admittedly stays on a surface level. Those familiar with the depth of Jung's work, as well as the Myers-Briggs Type Indicator, know there is tremendous complexity and richness that comes from going deeper into how other psychological functions influence our introversion (read *Please Understand Me* by David Keirsey and Marilyn Bates to learn more).[5] It's dangerous to generalize and say something is or isn't true for all introverts. Remember as you read this book, or any book about introversion or personality, you will find as many descriptions to be true as not true. There are introverts who love to network, go through a sales process, or make speeches with no preparation. There are others who dread those activities but want to develop those skills in service to their vision. Wherever you fall on the spectrum, there will be times when your introversion will be a strength and other times when it will be a challenge. Your power lies in your awareness and the degree to which you act on that awareness.

Most people fall fairly clearly on one side or the other on the introvert–extrovert scale. That said, we all have elements of both energies within us. It's simply a matter of which is more dominant. Introverts have a side of them that is outgoing, energized by interaction, and likes to talk through challenges to work them out. Extroverts have a side that needs to rest, reflect, and recharge through quiet time and solitude. You can generally tell which one is dominant by which one is your default. There is generally one type of energy-boosting activity—solitude or socializing—that is your preference and to which you're naturally drawn.

Interestingly, I often hear people observe that they've become more introverted as they've matured. Perhaps they don't feel the need to perform or prove themselves anymore, or they've had their fill of parties. Perhaps they're responding to—and wanting to step away from—the overstimulation that is rampant in our society. Whatever the reason, it's anecdotal evidence that while we are predisposed to being more introverted or extroverted, it's possible that the scales may tip as we age.

One point I want to make crystal clear: Claiming the word *introvert* is not about slapping a label on you or putting you into a little box. It's about having another piece of information that can help you understand yourself better, be true to yourself, and along the way create a successful and sustainable business.

Other introvert traits and preferences include the following (this is a generalized list; there are as many different variations and levels of introversion as there are introverts):

- Thinking carefully before speaking or acting
- Preferring to express feelings in writing rather than talking
- Having a selected few deep, close friendships
- Disliking small talk
- Enjoying self-reflection and introspection
- Having different public and private personas

Split Personality?

That last one on the list trips people up the most. Being an introvert is not always an obvious personality trait. Introverts don't wear a scarlet *I* on their clothing. They commonly refer to needing to put on an extrovert hat or mask during the day while they're working, then retreating when they're not. It's not that they're a split personality or that what you see in public is not the "real" person. It's simply that over time, many introverts have learned to manage their energy to match the situation. They know how to be social or spontaneous and still take care of themselves and their needs.

It's undeniably a balancing act; we have certain preferences and tendencies that have the potential to get in our way as we move out into a predominantly extroverted world.

In fact, it's estimated that 50 percent of the population is introverted.[6] So why do introverts feel like we're in the minority?

The dominant culture (at least in the United States) favors extroverted behaviors. We're constantly pressured to be social: go to parties; make lots of friends; be funny, smart, and the life of the party. And if you're an entrepreneur or a midlevel manager of a start-up who's expected to act entrepreneurially, the pressure is intensified. We're told that we need to engage in constant business development if we want to be successful. That means much of our time is spent with networking, self-promotion, collaboration, public speaking, selling, selling, and more selling.

As we move through the various aspects of being an introvert entrepreneur, we'll spend time going into more detail around each of these areas. Before we do that, let's explore an area that introverts often think they aren't very good in but that can actually be an incredible entrepreneurial asset: communication.

Measure Twice, Cut Once

> *Calvin: Sometimes when I'm talking, my words can't keep up with my thoughts. I wonder why we think faster than we speak.*
>
> *Hobbes: Probably so we can think twice.*
> —Bill Watterson, *Calvin and Hobbes*

So often, when relationships break down, everyone points the finger of blame in one direction: to communication, or rather, the lack thereof. The exchange between Calvin and Hobbes highlights perfectly why there are so many problems: Our thoughts and our speech don't always align in a way that pleases everyone.

The reasons for crossed signals and misunderstandings are numerous and complex. It would be too simple to say that the root of it all lies in the difference between how introverts and extroverts communicate. However, much of the friction—and fiction—that comes from poor communication could be alleviated if we all had a basic understanding of how we each think and speak.

As we learned earlier, introverts gain energy from solitude and drain energy from too much social interaction. In contrast, extroverts gain energy from being around and interacting with other people; being alone for too long is tedious and boring.

Another key point of differentiation between these two personality types is how they process information, which in turn influences how they interact with others.

Introverts are internal processors. Their primary source of information and point of reference comes from within themselves. This doesn't mean that they are self-absorbed or oblivious to others; they simply rely first and foremost on their inner thoughts to guide them. For example, when an introvert receives information, she takes it in and flips it around in her mind until it's right side up enough to be shared with the world.

Extroverts rely more heavily on external stimulus to inform their views and choices. They tend to be verbal processors; rather than spending lots of time in quiet contemplation, they want to talk it out. When confronted with a challenge or decision, for example, the extrovert will pull in other people for brainstorming or discussion.

Translation, Please

> I know that you believe you understand what you think I said, but I'm not sure you realize that what you heard is not what I meant. —Robert McCloskey

You probably can see at least one way introvert–extrovert communication differences cause problems in the workplace or at home. Let's consider a common occurrence: An extrovert manager wants to call a team meeting to solve a problem that's just surfaced. Within that team, there is a mixture of introverts and extroverts. The manager decides to have a freewheeling discussion about the problem, expecting to act immediately after the meeting.

The extroverts dive right in, brainstorming and thinking aloud. There is little to no time lapse between their thought and their speech. Meanwhile, the introverts are taking in the information and turning it over in their minds, thinking through various scenarios and solutions. Before they even say a word, they may have considered and dismissed several ideas. Rather than talk stream-of-consciousness, they wait until they have a fully formed idea before speaking.

In the meantime, the manager has moved on, the extroverts have all had their say, and the meeting comes to an end. The introverts may or may not have gotten to chime in (they prefer not to interrupt; better to ask them what they think), and so several of them choose to have one-on-one conversations with the manager or key people after the meeting.

While the extroverts are like Calvin in the opening quote—leading with speech rather than thoughts—the introverts are like Hobbes and thinking twice.

Put another way, introverts tend to measure twice and cut once.

This can lead to impatience on the part of both personality types. Extroverts want introverts to think and speak up faster; introverts want extroverts to slow down and leave space for more thinking. Without understanding that these tendencies are about as hardwired as brown eyes or blond hair, people can go through life thinking introverts are withholding and slow and extroverts are nonstop blabbermouths.

Closing the Communication Gap

While a zebra can't change its stripes, it can adapt to its environment enough to survive and thrive. Here are a few quick tips to help smooth things out when communication gets a little rocky.

When talking to introverts:

- Give them adequate time to think through a question or problem. If at all possible, don't put them on the spot and demand an immediate answer.

- Offer to provide as much advance information as possible about a situation and be prepared to answer questions. Introverts like to both be prepared and clear about expectations. Ask if written information is preferred (too much out-loud sharing might be overstimulating).
- You may find that you need to intentionally call on introverts in group discussions. Ask, "Do you have anything you'd like to add?" or "Joe, what do you think?" Avoid calling attention to their relative silence with, "You're awfully quiet over there." Chances are the introvert is quiet externally because he's actively listening and forming a response in his head. Don't compose elaborate stories, make assumptions, or read anything into his silence; just ask.
- Get comfortable with pauses, longer silences, and nonverbal cues. The pace of a conversation with an introvert feels different because she's thinking before she speaks. Once she does start talking, refrain from interrupting or finishing her sentences.

When talking to extroverts:

- Give them time and space to process out loud, and be patient with the faster energy that they project. This is how they come to conclusions.
- Listen carefully and be prepared to interrupt if you need to make a point. Extroverts aren't necessarily going to pause or make room for you. Jump in as needed and use body language to reinforce your point.
- Understand that extroverts speak to think. They may change their mind after some time away from a conversation; be ready for that possibility.

- Be aware that they make decisions based on external feedback, so be direct and forthcoming. Give feedback in a way that feels comfortable to you and that the extrovert can absorb.
- Ask them what information they need. Most likely, it's a broad overview or summary of the situation rather than lots of depth or details.

Understanding and respecting differences in communication style is essential to building positive and productive relationships. Without that understanding, we can personalize, make assumptions, and misinterpret what another person is saying. Patience is important, as is allowing space for someone to say, "You know, I need time to think about this, and then I'll get back to you," or "It would really help me to be able to talk this through, and you just listen."

When we know what works for us, we can ask for what we want. And sometimes that's all that's needed to keep bad communication from happening in the first place.

Strengths of the Introvert Entrepreneur

Introverts, rejoice! You are about to learn about some of the most fabulous parts of your personality, just waiting to be unleashed on the world. I like to call them your "secret superpowers." Why secret? Because the extroverted society we live in moves so quickly and loudly that our superpowers are often working quietly behind the scenes and under the radar, unseen by others.

Here's the truth: Some of the most famous, wealthy, and successful people on the planet are introverts. And it's their super-powers that helped them get there.

Consider these household names: Bill Gates, Warren Buffett, and Charles Schwab. Steven Spielberg, Michael Jordan, and Julia Roberts. We don't think of these people as shy underachievers, do we? Yet, they all identify themselves as introverts. There are also the introvert founders of some of the most successful social networking sites: Mark Zuckerberg (Facebook), Jack Dorsey (Twitter), and Larry Page (Google). And while I haven't come across definitive proof, many signs point to President Barack Obama being a member of Team Introvert.

What these people have in common is that they have channeled their introvert strengths into superpowers that enable them to succeed in a noisy world. How do they do that? By recognizing those strengths in the first place.

Working from the definition that introverts are focused on gaining energy and insight from the reality of the internal self (as opposed to external realities), I've identified four introvert "self" strengths that contribute to our success:

- Self-effacing
- Self-reliant
- Self-possessed
- Self-reflective

As you read the following descriptions, think about how the strengths show up for you and how they support your professional goals. You might be surprised to realize that traits you take for granted could be the keys to helping you stand out and lead the pack.

Self-Effacing

Introverts don't tend to be divas. Many times, we don't even like to be in the spotlight. But that doesn't mean we're necessarily shy or that we dislike being in leadership positions. Instead, we can take heart in the description of Level 5 Leadership by Jim Collins, author of *Good to Great*. A Level 5 leader is characterized by Collins and his team as embodying "a paradoxical mix of personal humility and professional will. They are ambitious, to be sure, but ambitious first and foremost for the company, not themselves."

Level 5 leaders also "display compelling modesty, are self-effacing and understated." Other words that describe them include *quiet, dogged, humble, shy, reserved, modest, gracious, calm*, and *shares or deflects the credit*.

Do those words sound familiar?

They should, because they are often the traits associated with introverts!

While Collins never uses the word *introvert* to describe them, his studies reflect a compelling consistency of introverted traits showing up in Level 5 leaders. This suggests that introverts have the capacity to be extraordinary leaders.

Self-Reliant

Because introverts look internally for our energy sources, we are often our own best friend. We don't depend on material or external stimulation to make up our mind about certain things or to recharge our batteries. It's not that we aren't influenced by our environment or the people around us; we simply take in the information and put it through our own filters rather than taking it at face value. We carry our safety, our values, and our energy around inside of us, which contributes to an unmistakable quality of independence and self-reliance.

My guess is that whoever coined the phrase "If you want it done right, do it yourself" was an introvert!

Ralph Waldo Emerson's "Self-Reliance" essay includes numerous statements about the virtues of this introvert tendency. Here's one example: "It is easy in the world to live after the world's opinion; it is easy in solitude to live after our own; but the great man is he who in the midst of the crowd keeps with perfect sweetness the independence of solitude."

Self-Possessed

The self-possessed superpower goes hand in hand with self-reliance. The *Collins English Dictionary* defines the term *self-possessed* as "having or showing control of one's feelings, behavior, etc.; composed; poised." For introverts, it specifically means that we are in full possession of our thoughts and feelings.

To refer back to Jim Collins and Level 5 Leadership, the most effective leaders were seen as calm and in control of their emotions, thoughts, and actions. Introverts process information internally rather than thinking out loud. By leaving space for this and allowing our thoughts to possess us for a time, introverts can remain calm in the midst of chaos and respond thoughtfully to even the most stressful situations.

Self-Reflective

If you're an introvert, you've probably heard someone say, "You think too much!" more than once in your life. I know I have! And yet, that willingness to reflect and turn inward to listen to my heart is a strength I wouldn't trade for anything.

It's not that extroverts don't engage in self-reflection or that introverts always trust their gut; it's more about the first reaction someone has to solving a problem. The extrovert will want to gather others and reflect collectively, to ask, "What do you think?" The introvert will move toward solitude or maybe one other person, to ask, "What do I think?" Both are using information from others to enlighten their thoughts. The introvert prefers to reflect on that information by going deeper into the self rather than assembling the troops.

The self-reflective superpower also shows up in how we respond to new situations. I sum it up by saying we like to look before we leap. Life is full of sayings that encourage us to "just do it." Consider this quote from French writer Nicolas de Chamfort: "Contemplation often makes life miserable. We should act more, think less, and stop watching ourselves live."

Telling introverts to sacrifice reflection is like asking us to stop breathing. We like to watch a bit before jumping into the fray. We are measuring expectations, norms, and rules. While this may sometimes get in our way (it's important to be aware if we're suffering from paralysis by analysis!), it's often the thing that saves us, and rescues many situations from being worsened by quick and rash responses.

Introverts watch. We wait. We act when the time feels right. Recognize that your desire and need to reflect is a secret superpower that will help you to be in the right place at the right time, ready with the right response.

These are only a few examples of the strengths introverts bring to the table. As we move through each of the major aspects of being an introvert entrepreneur, we'll highlight additional strengths and explore how to use them. You'll find advice that will support you wherever you are in your professional journey, whether you are the owner of a business, are part of a larger start-up, or have an entrepreneurial role in a traditional corporation or nonprofit organization. As you understand, own, and leverage your introvert strengths, new opportunities will present themselves. Doors will open. The world will be a better place because of your thoughtful, internal power.

Challenges and Considerations of the Introvert Entrepreneur

There is a flip side to the strengths; almost any of them can be turned around and become exactly the thing that holds you back from success. While everyone with an entrepreneurial mindset has concerns and challenges as they embark on their journey, there are certain areas that are worth extra attention for the introvert. You'll find these themes addressed directly, as well as in the context of other areas, throughout this book.

Finding Your Voice

Until recently, being an introvert was something that most people didn't want to embrace; they wanted to fix it. The messages that it's not OK to be an introvert meant that many people spent enormous amounts of energy trying to be extroverted. The result? Besides some very tired, burned-out introverts, we had people whose voices were not ringing true.

An introvert entrepreneur needs to be clear from the start on several things: values, purpose, goals, and vision. From that clarity comes the ability to own who you are, thereby claiming your unique voice and marketplace niche. One of my favorite writers (who also happens to be an introvert), Anne Lamott, has said that part of the meaning of life is reclaiming your truth, the one that others twist or mute on our journey toward social acceptability. Our truth is discovered when we're quiet and when we embrace what's true for us, not what's true for someone else.

Networking

You're an introvert entrepreneur, and you're excited about what you have to offer. You've outlined your services, set up your website, printed business cards, established a few promotions, and taken care of all the legalities to make your business official. You can do all of this from the comfort and safety of your home or office, away from people asking you questions and giving you advice. But there comes the day when you have to step outside and into the public eye. You realize that people don't buy from websites or promotional flyers; they buy from people. That means you have to see and be seen on a regular basis, which means networking. Lots and lots of networking.

One of the reasons why networking ranks high on the discomfort index is because it usually involves large events with people we don't know; it only facilitates short conversations and quick connections; and in general, it's a huge energy drain. I've heard lots of introverts proclaim, "I hate networking!" or "I'm not good at networking," statements that only make the entire experience more stressful. However, it's an indispensable business development activity, so we might as well learn to do it in a way that aligns with our strengths. We'll cover this in more detail in Chapter 4.

Self-Promotion

Talking about ourselves is a close runner-up with networking on the introvert discomfort index. We usually prefer to deflect the focus onto other people or topics so that we can maintain some level of personal reserve. After all, if we have to talk about ourselves, we're bringing what was previously internal and making it external, which means it's open to judgment, scrutiny, and misunderstanding. Because we live from the inside out, we're especially aware of the ramifications of sharing our inner world.

Anne Lamott says we all embody the conflicting traits of self-loathing and narcissism. Our self-loathing—not because we're introverts but because we're human—is part of what might hold us back when it's time to self-promote. Our narcissism pulls us toward making a mark in the world, something that says, "I was here and I want you to know it and to know it was *me*." When it comes to self-promotion, we want to achieve a balance between those contradictory traits. Healthy self-loathing might show up as humility or self-effacement. Healthy narcissism can manifest as positive energy and confidence that we can and will accomplish our goals.

Energy Management

As we've explored earlier, being an introvert is largely about how we gain and drain energy. The business development activities of networking and self-promotion have the potential to be the biggest energy drains of all. They require a level of social presence and being "on" that does not come naturally to the average introvert. We have to extrovert (as a verb—we don't have to *become* an extrovert) and develop a personal presence that is both genuine and powerful. To be out and about, we have to go inward and nowhere, recharging our batteries so that we have enough energy to make it through the next event or meeting. It's not always easy to find the downtime, especially if we're working out of the home. Our home life and work life bleeds together with no distinguishable boundary.

The beginning years find us working 24/7, sitting at the computer, going to events, or composing blog posts in our heads while we empty the dishwasher or put in another load of laundry. Social media adds another wrinkle into the mix; we might not be physically in front of people all day, but we are interacting constantly on Facebook, Twitter, LinkedIn, Google+, Pinterest, and any number of virtual platforms that constantly bring LOL and IMHO voices into our quiet headspace. There's also the issue of too much alone time. Just as too much social interaction drains us, our batteries can be depleted if we are too isolated or left alone with only virtual voices and our own mind chatter for too long. So it's critical that we be intentional and creative about managing our energy if we want to build a successful and sustainable business.

Isolation and Collaboration

As an introvert entrepreneur, you probably have a strong independent streak and may even take pride in considering yourself a jack- or jill-of-all-trades. You may have even gone into business to escape the more team-driven corporate environment, and you relish the time you spend working alone. There comes a time, however, when you realize that you need to pull in other people, whether they are employees, contractors, coaches, or project partners. These people can step in to assist with areas that aren't your strength. Or perhaps they enhance and broaden your expertise to take your message to a new market.

Collaboration is another area that can either boost or drain your energy, depending on how thoughtfully you enter into it. During the collaboration itself, it's essential to establish a trusting relationship, built on transparency and proactive communication. Introvert entrepreneurs need to be especially attentive to knowing how to identify a prime opportunity, how to establish clear roles and responsibilities, and how to balance the more social aspect of collaboration with the need for solo work time.

Personal and Professional Sustainability

There's a lot of talk these days about sustainability in the environment. If you think of your business as its own environment, are you making professional choices that support sustainability? And even more important for you as an introvert, are you making personal choices that support sustainability?

Even if you feel strong in some of these typically challenging areas, there's always room for growth. I once heard professional keynote speaker Patricia Fripp share this advice, which applies to both speaking and building a business: Having natural talent is great, but when you pair it with lots of practice and continuous skill improvement, you're unstoppable.

Introvert Entrepreneur Focus

Laurie Helgoe, PhD, psychologist, assistant professor
of psychology, Davis & Elkins College, and author of
Introvert Power: Why Your Inner Life Is Your Hidden Strength

There's a perception that introverts are depressed or perpetually melancholy because we don't always appear outwardly happy as society has defined it. How do we break that stereotype?

What we talk about in our culture as happiness is really kind of a revved-up version of happiness. It's a high-energy [state]—scientists call it a high-arousal positive affect. It's a feeling, it's transient, it's not quality of life, it's not so many things.

And it doesn't leave room for an entire set of positive emotions that are of a calmer variety, expressed by words like *serene, calm, tranquil, relaxed*. I find it fascinating that these low-arousal positive feelings are more valued than the high-arousal ones in other societies, such as China [and] Japan, more collectivistic cultures. So we take an extrovert in our society, she's going to feel better about herself than an extrovert in one of these collectivistic societies. It's really important for us to start to look at the ways we narrow our definition of what is happy.

Introverts are known for their love of solitude; I often think of it as one of my happy places. Do you think we can ever get too much of a good thing?

There's a lot of wonderful poetry about solitude, but sometimes solitude sucks and sometimes it's not this rich, wonderful space. Just like we get into small talk when we're in social situations, we can get into small thoughts sometimes when we're alone. I've found that it's very important to feed our solitude and nourish it by being selective about what we watch and what we read and take into that space.

What do you appreciate most about being an introvert?

I like that my mind wants to make up stories and observe. When I travel, I love the experience of being a *flâneur*—which we don't really have an adequate translation for—the passionate observer, somebody who can be in the midst of things and not a part of them but observe and just take in the energy of the surroundings in a quieter way. Just being one step removed can be just a wonderful place to be.

Chapter 2

Fear, Doubt, and Other Icky Stuff Most Entrepreneurs Don't Want to Talk About

"Fear has held my business success back more than anything else. It's taken (and is still taking) years to overcome it."

"The more we talk about it [fear], the less power it has over us."

"I think as introverts we are our own worst critics."

"Fear is the one obstacle that I keep coming up against in trying to develop my business. I am very conscious of this, and I fight it every day—fear of rejection, fear of success, etc."

Along with a chorus of thumbs-up, the epigraphs that open this chapter are some of the responses I received when I shared on Facebook that I felt compelled to write about fear—a topic not often addressed directly in traditional business books. Every one of them hit home with me, but it was Claudine Motto, owner of Business in Blossom, whose words resonated with me the most. She shared that the biggest obstacle to productivity wasn't Facebook,

Twitter, Pinterest, or email, and it wasn't that we lack the perfect organizer or filing system or a faster, fancier laptop. It's the one thing that costs nothing but still costs us everything: *fear*.

This is where the rubber hits the road. Introverts are pros at thinking and planning, scheming and dreaming . . . and at some point, all of what's been going on inside of us, or has only been living on our laptop, has to come out. It has to be born. It can't stay in the safe, protected place where everything turns out exactly how we want it to and everyone flocks to buy what we have to offer.

It's all well and good that we know our values, truth, and purpose; as we'll explore in Chapter 3, that's the hard-core stuff that separates the entrepreneurial wannabes from the people who actualize their vision. And, if there's anything that's going to get in the way during our quiet march to success, it's fear. We might decide that the reason we fail to make progress is because the sheer volume of work and energy output overwhelms us. We don't have enough clients, customers, time, resources, or money to keep going, it's a bad economy, or even because we're introverts. (More on that point in Chapter 5.) But there's no getting around it. Under every excuse, behind every story, is fear, plain and simple.

If we don't allow ourselves to acknowledge fear, we're going to stumble, again and again. Even the most confident, outgoing people experience fear. Being smart, thoughtful, and focused does not make you immune to fear. In this chapter, I invite you to set aside any pressure to be fearless and let yourself be human.

The amount of fear you feel is not directly related to whether you're an introvert or extrovert. I don't think introverts experience any more or less fear . . . what's different is our *relationship* to the fear. We relate first to our inner world, which means we are more likely to sit in fear alone for a while. Left to its own devices, fear will occupy valuable real estate in our minds, bouncing around in what my colleague Judy Dunn refers to as our "echo chamber."

> *Courage is resistance to fear, mastery of fear, not absence of fear.*
> —Mark Twain

The Flaw with Being Fearless

In 2010, I attended the outstanding Grow Your Business Expo sponsored by the *Puget Sound Business Journal* in Seattle. Exhibitors and presenters all focused on providing helpful resources and strategies to entrepreneurs, and they did a great job. As the day went on, however, I noticed a common theme among many of the speakers: *Be fearless!*

Every time someone said that, I cringed inside.

When we discussed that day what's most needed in business, the answer was to *be fearless!* When doubts creep in, we're supposed to *be fearless!* And the best way to get over our fears is to *be fearless!*

Hogwash!

What's Wrong with the Pep-Rally Approach

I understand that the people who say *be fearless!* have only the best intentions. They don't mean to be flippant or to dishonor my feelings. And for some who hear them, those words inspire them to step up and take action. The phrase reminds them that they can choose to let fear get in the way or they can kick it to the curb.

For me, though, *be fearless!* is like a pep-rally slogan that fires up my energy just in time for the big game, but then leaves me stranded at the end. I feel a momentary boost of energy and courage, and that might last me a few days. It's like I've had a shot of caffeine and can face the world again. Eventually, though, the buzz wears off. If I continually use this technique to vanquish my fear— just pep-talking my way out of it—the fear will knock again, letting me know it's not finished with me yet. Eventually, it will kick down the door.

Why is that? Did it not hear me when I said, "Go away"? It heard me, but that particular fear represents a part of me that feels vulnerable and wants to protect me, which is a strong motivator for paying attention to it.

Think about the fears you've experienced. Chances are high that most of them—if not all—were trying to stop you from doing something that could expose you to failure or humiliation. Even though it doesn't feel like it, the fear has your best interests at heart. So it's going to knock again, louder this time. It wants to make sure it has your attention.

Your reaction to it this time might be to feel even more frustration or fear because you thought you'd shaken off the fear at the pep rally, and you realize you're no more equipped to deal with it now than you were the first time around. You haven't stopped shouting down the fear long enough to be curious about what's really going on.

Introverts are internally motivated; our boost comes from the inside out, and we're only minimally influenced by the pep-rally approach, which is a superficial rah-rah-rah mentality that bombards us from the outside.

"Admit the fear," advises Betsy Talbot, founder of Married with Luggage. She told me:

I like to maintain a certain level of public composure, but I realize now how hard it is if you have no outlet for your fears and frustrations. I have an inner circle of people with whom I can share these fears without judgment and get the kind of feedback and support to help me move forward.

As an introvert I don't like to make myself vulnerable to other people, but I've found that when I do, I always come out better on the other side . . . and so does my business. It's why I'm admitting my fear to you as the author of this book. The fear doesn't ever go away, but how I handle it evolves as I do.

While *be fearless!* is a common theme in the business world, the entrepreneurial theme that works well for me and my introverted clients is the title of Susan Jeffers's book: *Feel the Fear and Do It Anyway.*

Letting Fear Be Seen and Heard

Feel the fear and do it anyway recognizes that fear exists. The phrase helps us move through our introvert desire to fly solo, to limit networking to the bare minimum, and to stay quiet when we ought to speak up. We can still honor our fear by acknowledging it and feeling *into* it. By taking that step, we gain valuable information about how to move forward with more confidence and self-compassion.

When we allow the fear to be seen and heard, we're also quicker to notice when we're making up excuses (including playing the introvert card). We know on an intellectual level that such excuses are protecting us from being hurt by keeping us in a safe, comfortable place, where we know where everything is and how things are going to turn out. *But these excuses don't keep us safe; they keep us small.*

Excuses mean we are approaching the inevitable challenges in our lives from a place of fear rather than love. This fear-based approach can easily carry over into our business. It can sabotage our best intentions if we don't identify the source of our excuses.

Are You Coming from Fear or Love?

At the root of every excuse is fear. As Wayne Dyer points out in his book *Excuses Begone!*, there are really only two emotions: fear and love. Here's how I see it: If we were coming from a place of love—for ourselves, for others, for our purpose, for our existence as a representation of the divine—then there would be no place for excuses (that is, fear). The excuses are simply a way to put a label on the fear.

Sometimes fear is a powerful motivator, much more potent than love. We're moved to take action based on feelings of scarcity or because we're seeking to avoid something. In our personal lives, it might sound like "I need to lose weight because if I'm too fat, my spouse will leave me." That gets us off the couch and onto the treadmill, but the negative feelings are more likely to linger even after we lose the weight, making us fearful our spouse will still leave us for some other reason.

In our entrepreneurial lives, we'll tell ourselves, Take the prospecting call or lose a potential new client. Say yes to the project that doesn't fit my business just because it will bring in some much-needed income. Don't tell my client that I need a deadline extension because I work better under pressure.

The voice of fear-based motivation isn't always this obvious. I hear it at times during coaching sessions. I'll ask a client, "What's motivating you?" or "What do you want?" And the answer starts with a negative: "I don't want to . . ." It's important to know what you don't want. That said, if you stop at that awareness, you'll be making choices based on moving away from something (fear) instead of moving toward something (love).

One of my favorite quotes of all time is an Old English proverb that says, "Fear knocked on the door. Love answered, and no one was there."

It's a magical image for me. It acknowledges that fear knocks. All the time. Every day. And then it shows me that by answering with love, the fear will fade (at least until it's ready to come knocking again!).

So telling me to be fearless is not recognizing and honoring my flawed humanity. A friend taught me this lesson early in my coaching career. We were having a phone conversation in which she was sharing her challenges with building her business. She was feeling really down about things, and I could hear fear and doubt creeping into her voice. I said something to the effect of, "Well, what if you thought about it this way?" and offered a chipper, turn-that-frown-upside-down suggestion. My friend, much to her credit, politely but firmly rejected my offer. "I want to feel better eventually, but right now, I need to just be afraid. I need to feel what I feel. If you tell me to just perk up, that doesn't help."

By trying to fix her fear, I was failing to acknowledge that fear serves a purpose. Telling me to be fearless does not give me or anyone else the space to feel what we feel.

Susan "Joy" Schleef of Presentations with Results shares this about her experience with fear: "Fears and doubts are a normal part of every life. Pushing them away, denying them, or trying to squelch them only works in the short term. When they come back later, they are often bigger and feel even scarier! If I accept them, feel them, and breathe through them, they usually pass fairly quickly."

Rather than try to be fearless, I prefer to lean into the fear (just a little, not enough to fall down), acknowledge it, and then challenge it. If I can't find a way to change the situation, then I change my attitude about the situation by tapping into the part of me that's motivated by love.

What does it mean to answer with love? First, acknowledge that you feel the fear in the first place. Let it be what it's going to be. Then notice what the fear is challenging. What button is being pushed? Is it your self-identity? Your reputation? Your closely held beliefs? Your plans for your business? Your relationships?

There's a reason why the fear has so much power: You care deeply about whatever is being threatened. You care what happens to your business. You care about living in alignment with your core values. You care about the people you've chosen to have in your life. Bring up in your mind what's most important to you about those aspects of your life. Let those feelings rise to the surface. What would they say, if those feelings based in love could talk to the fear? If the fear is there to protect you from being hurt, then what is the compassionate response? It might be as simple as saying, "Fear, I hear you. I know you're trying to keep me from failing or getting hurt. I trust that I can handle this."

At its core, responding with love means you're responding from a place of trust and peace rather than fear and anxiety. It means getting in touch not with just what's going on but why it matters to you. Your "why" might be your values, your vision, or your dream.

"When in doubt, tune into your heart to find the big why," says the Black Swan coach Val Nelson. "If your heart still says no, that path might not be aligned with you. Thus you learn to distinguish fear from inner wisdom. The heart knows."

So far we've talked about the internal approach to changing our relationship to fear. But the remedy you use to help you shift your perspective doesn't have to be mental. While introverts tend to be internally motivated, it also helps to consider how we learn and remember things. Are you a visual, auditory, or kinesthetic learner? Depending on your style, different triggers will have more meaning for you. For instance, photographer Colleen Carroll has a tangible reminder of what motivates her. She says, "I have a talisman that I carry with me, a heart that fits in the palm of my hand carved with the word *love*. It reminds me that my passion is stronger than my fears."

You might enjoy listening to affirmations or a meditation before going to sleep each night. I have a few pick-me-up songs that fill me with a sense of purpose and power. Some people appreciate visual cues such as posters, plaques, or statues that remind them of a favorite quote or inspirational figure. It doesn't really matter what form the affirmation comes in; what's most important is that you find something that's meaningful and centering to you.

This process of looking your fear in the face is not always easy. It might not tell you what you want to hear. After all, what if, as Val says, the heart says no? The benefit to the introvert entrepreneur is that we don't waste time, energy, and resources barreling down a path that's not right for us. We've learned to trust our internal barometer and give power to our inner wisdom, not our fear.

Fear and Scarcity: Mind over Chatter and the Overactive Introvert Brain

The pathway is smooth. Why do you throw rocks before you?
—Ancient sage wisdom

Imagine that your business is a path of your own making. How smooth is the road under your feet? If you listen too much to the media and people who are talking from a fear-based perspective, your road may become littered with rocks and obstacles, each one with a different label: Poor economy. Challenging cash flow. Sales. Bankruptcy. Struggle. Scarcity. Certainly, there are obstacles over which you have no control. However, when we look down the road with a critical eye, we clearly see that many of the things tripping us up are rocks we've tossed there ourselves.

The role that fear plays in our lives is so common that it's been used by marketers for decades. For instance, FUD, a term credited to Gene Amdahl, who worked for IBM during the 1980s, stands for fear, uncertainty, and doubt.[1] Amdahl developed a marketing strategy that trained the sales force to instill fear, uncertainty, and doubt in the minds of its customers in regard to switching products. "Stick with IBM. We're big, we're safe, you know what you're getting. If you go with another company, anything could happen, and you might not like it." The technique was subsequently employed by Microsoft and has reared its ugly head in the political arena, too.

FUDs turn up not only in marketing and politics but in how we approach our role as introvert entrepreneurs. If we get real with ourselves, we can admit that underneath the positive talk, confident face, and outgoing energy that we try to project to our colleagues, family, and friends, there are at least a few internal FUDs that we stumble over.

Identifying Your FUDs

While introverts aren't the only ones to experience FUDs, ours tend to share common themes that revolve around the vulnerability of making the internal external. Do any of these FUD rocks sound familiar?

- I'm too much of an introvert, too quiet for anyone to notice me in such a noisy marketplace.
- If I market too much, people will get annoyed with me.
- I can't handle rejection.
- What if my business fails and I let down my family?
- I'm not a good schmoozer and am terrible at sales.
- I'm showing up in all the right places and nothing's happening.
- I don't have the energy to keep putting myself out there.
- I'm not sure I can handle the push to keep going, going, going.

Some FUDs are pebbles, some are boulders. Even courageous, "fearless" people—whether they're introverts or extroverts—have to dodge FUD rocks on the road to success. What separates the people who keep moving from those who become tripped up by the rocks in their way? They recognize that *where they feel fear, there is energy.* There is something that wants attention. So they bring that energy—that feeling of fear—into conscious awareness.

One of the ways we can raise our awareness is to externalize the energy that's building up inside us. Joan Shulman of Full Circle Coaching reminds us that we don't have to go through that process alone. "When fear creeps in, reach out to someone who really hears you. Sharing our vulnerabilities with people we trust can bring the fear out from the darkness and into the light. Not so scary!"

Talking through the fears can highlight that the line between fear and excitement is very thin; the same adrenaline pumps through our bodies when we're afraid as when we're excited. The difference lies in how we choose to view the situation. Often, our perspective shifts more easily if we share our fears and doubts with someone else. From there, you can make the choice to channel the energy into action rather than internalize it and allow it to sabotage you.

Bringing Your FUDs Out into the Open

It's transformative to experience the power and clarity that comes when we're able to pull the FUDs off of the hamster wheel of our internal processing and into the light, where they rarely stand up to scrutiny. Do you want to know the truth about your FUDs? They want to be heard, and they think they are keeping you safe from failure. So giving them a voice is not about focusing on fear and negativity; it's about putting FUDs in their proper place—and out of your way—so you can focus on building your strengths.

Whether your FUDs are simply speed bumps on your journey or paralyzing you at every single turn, there's a way to work through them that helps convert the negative energy of fear into the positive energy of action. The following four steps provide a way to transform the fears into information that will move you forward:

1. Make a list of your FUDs.
2. Perform a reality check.
3. Realize you have choices.
4. Choose a prosperity perspective.

Make a List of Your FUDs

A good way to get all of your FUDs off the hamster wheel is to get them down on paper. Introverts are fabulous at thinking things through, but there comes a time when writing those thoughts down and externalizing them is important to your process. Write down the FUDs that are in your way in any area of your business. This may include marketing, finances, networking, an important decision, or the next big leap in your business.

Here are some fears, uncertainties, and doubts I've experienced or heard from introvert entrepreneur clients:

- If she wins, I lose.
- It's better to isolate, to keep ideas close to the vest.
- Small is safe.
- If I go to the event, I won't know what to say.
- I'm not cut out to sell myself or my ideas.

Do any of these sound familiar, or spark another idea for you?

Be as specific or as general as you want. Let it all out. List every FUD, no matter how large, trivial, scary, or petty it feels. Suspend judgment of yourself and your FUDs.

Release the FUDs to the paper and then don't think about them. Put the list away for the rest of the day (or week, if you prefer).

Perform a Reality Check

After you've gained some distance from your FUD list, you can approach it with a more objective eye. Review your list and look for two things: assumptions and limiting beliefs.

Assumptions are made either on past experience or future projections. They might sound like this:

"It's going to be difficult."
"I need a degree to do that."
"We can't afford that."
"I won't like it."
"We'd never get along."
"He probably hates me."
"Others will get hurt if I . . ."
"No one will help me."
"Everyone will think it's a silly idea."

Limiting beliefs are ways we make ourselves small by focusing on the negative, such as

"I'm not smart enough."
"I'm too old."
"I'm too fat."
"I'm only good at this one thing."
"You can't teach an old dog new tricks."
"I can either have this or that, not both."
"It's too late for me."

Many FUDs that pop up in business are assumptions: It's too hard to start a blog. No one is spending money. Others are most likely limiting beliefs: I've been in business only a year, so the only way I'll get new clients is if I give things away. Label each of your FUDs: either assumptions that need evidence or limiting beliefs that weigh you down.

Assumptions can be proven or disproven through honest self-reflection and evidence gathering. Once you have obtained evidence, you can make an informed choice based on reality.

For instance, let's take "We can't afford that." This one has popped up for me numerous times. For almost four years, I edited and produced my own podcasts. It was a time-consuming project, but I enjoyed the process, and I especially enjoyed having complete control. More important, I assumed that it would cost too much to contract with someone to assist me. Another assumption: Even if it didn't cost that much, I wouldn't have the money anyway. Finally one day, I reached the end of my rope. I had a backlog of podcasts and people waiting for their interviews to be posted. I posted the job on Elance.com and within an hour had eighteen freelance producers bidding on my project. And guess what? The investment they were asking for was a fraction of what I'd assumed! If I hadn't gathered the evidence, I'd have continued under the false assumption that contracting with someone wasn't an option. I would have continued to struggle along, alone, and not realizing that the money I spent on a contractor could be easily recovered (and then some) by the valuable revenue-generating time I freed up.

Limiting beliefs are often more personal in nature and require more soul searching. They arise from deep within, with their roots in past experiences. As such, they can appear to be larger than life. One quick way to right-size them is by challenging them with the question, "Is that true?" The answer is usually, "No, that's not entirely true." From that awareness, choices can emerge, and you'll find yourself well on your way to getting unstuck. (If you want to learn more about this idea, read the work of Byron Katie.)

What if you look at a FUD and think, "But that one's true"? Look deeper. *Is* it true? What evidence do you have? And if it really is true and an objective fact, is your fear about the truth itself or is it about your ability to handle or respond to that truth?

Realize You Have Choices

When we're caught in a Cycle of Fear, we often forget that we have choices. For instance, you might feel you have no choice but to do a project yourself because it would take too long to bring someone else in. You fear losing control of the situation. Contracting with someone equals headaches, right? But you want to reduce your stress.

What if there were other ways to accomplish that? There are other choices that can surface when you release the assumptions. Maybe you contract for support on only a specific part of the project. Or you extend the timetable. Or you decide to reduce its scope. Or you could decide to live with the stress, knowing it's short term. When FUDs are identified as assumptions or limiting beliefs, you're able to see more clearly that choices exist. Then you can decide how you're going to respond to each of your FUDs. Rather than accepting a particular solution by default and with a sense of powerlessness, you are intentionally choosing your response.

Choose a Prosperity Perspective

At the heart of a prosperity perspective is beginning to think in terms of "both/and," rather than "either/or." The latter places limiting beliefs around our situation: "I *either* start doing live events *or* I'll never reach new clients." Just as limiting is the "if/then" scenario; for example, "If I don't offer the lowest price, then people won't buy." When you catch yourself thinking in terms of if/ then or either/or statements, *stop.* Consider if what you're saying is really true.

At a minimum, those words are an indicator that you're cutting yourself off from choice. You're limiting your options. Let's look at the pricing example: There is truth to the idea that if your prices aren't low enough, people won't buy. But that's not the *only* truth. There's also the possibility that:

- If your prices are too low, people will devalue your product; can what you have to offer be good if it's that cheap?
- If you start low and train clients or customers to expect low prices, it'll be difficult to raise them later.
- If you start higher, you can always offer discounts later.
- You're starting with low prices because you have doubts about your value. If you doubt it, others will as well.
- You can find a midrange of price points that stretch both you and your customer in a positive way.

Once you start recognizing the other possibilities, you have lessened the power that fear has over you. You might still decide to lower your price; but in that case, the decision to do so is based on thoughtful reflection and strategy rather than fear. There's a big difference in the way that feels to you and comes across to your market.

From this vantage point, there is more than enough of everything you need and want for your business and success. Choice has replaced fear.

Shift your energy and choose excitement over fear. Commit to a new perspective. Recall what I shared earlier about the purpose of fear and what happens if we ignore it: It will keep coming back—*knock, knock, KNOCK*—until we acknowledge it. For example, you could say: "FUD, I hear you and know that you're trying to protect me from risk and failure. Thank you for your concern. I've thought about what you said, and my intention going forward is to place a high value on what I have to offer, show up with enthusiasm, and enroll two new clients this month."

Write down your new commitments and integrate them into your vision for your business or action plan. Include your intention along with each action step so that you keep front and center why you are not willing to give in to your assumptions and limiting beliefs. Let's say you have an outline for a local, live workshop you eventually want to go national. You're struggling to come up with just the right price point, and you're afraid if you set it too high, people won't come. Yet, you also want the workshop and any products that come out of it to account for 25 percent of your annual revenue.

Now consider these questions: What is your overall intention for the first workshop? What do you want to experience? What do you want your participants to experience? What seeds do you want to be planting? Taking those questions into account, your intention might sound like this: "With this first workshop, I intend to deliver a high-quality, information-rich experience for my attendees. I want to learn about their needs more clearly so I can create an expanded offering for more people in the future." Given that intention, the pricing dilemma takes a backseat to the experience. Being grounded in your vision and intention takes some of the power away from the fear around money. This makes it a bit easier to listen to your inner wisdom around what's most important and what will move you to action—and a price you feel good about—rather than keeping you stuck in the fear.

When you try this four-step process on your own, it may not be as clear-cut as it appears here. And for the commitment to translate into results, you will need to develop an action plan. It's helpful to work through this process with a coach, mentor, or trusted colleague. We're sometimes too close to the FUDs; the thought patterns are deep-rooted, and our emotions keep us from being objective enough to see where scarcity thinking is showing up and manifesting itself. I recommend you find someone you trust, with whom you feel completely safe, to support you through the process.

On the road to prosperity and intention, there will always be a few pebble FUDs, and maybe the occasional boulder. They show up because we're human, and sometimes we need to vent and have something to kick or throw around. But at least now we recognize what's happening and have a process to help shift our energy.

Knowing the Difference Between Fear and Discomfort

One key to taking control over your FUDs is knowing how to distinguish fear from discomfort. Discomfort is a feeling of uneasiness or distress. It's often just the residual ickiness that fear leaves behind, and the only way to wash it off is to move into action.

The *Random House Dictionary* defines *discomfort* as "an absence of comfort or ease; uneasiness, hardship, or mild pain." There are plenty of times in our entrepreneurial journey when we'll feel an absence of comfort. Comfort is sending an email; discomfort is picking up the phone. Comfort is skipping happy hour after the conference sessions; discomfort is stopping in for a while.

Those activities might induce mild discomfort, but that's different from outright fear. Fear is "a distressing emotion aroused by impending danger, evil, pain, etc., whether the threat is real or imagined" (per the *Random House Dictionary*).

We often collapse the labels of fear and discomfort. We use them to describe the same feeling (not unlike how people collapse introvert and shy). But if we tease them apart, there's a big difference between something causing uneasiness and something being dangerous or evil. There is no danger in picking up the phone or attending the event. No great evil will emerge if you speak up in front of the group or initiate a conversation with a prospect.

When I put it that way, it almost sounds silly to label those feelings as fears. It's not. In the moment, you might be experiencing a true fight-or-flight response. The idea is to question the emotion and sit with it a bit: Is it truly fear or is it discomfort? Do you actually feel threatened or simply uncomfortable?

It might not appear to be a particularly profound distinction, but I've found for my clients and me, it's important. There's a big difference in the way it feels to say "I'm terrified of networking" and "Networking is uncomfortable for me." One sounds like a relatively unalterable state, and the other like something that can be moved through or transformed. After all, any time you're doing something new, you're liable to experience discomfort. If you give yourself credit for all of the discomforts you work through on a daily basis, you're well on your way to knowing that you can handle it.

Remember: Fear is primal, and thus requires more reflection and time to transcend it. But a word of caution: Sitting with the fear does not mean overthinking it. As Claudine Motto shares, "I can overanalyze situations and have to jolt myself into making decisions. I work very hard to stay aware of that and make a conscious effort to identify which problems or situations deserve careful thinking and research and consideration, and which do not."

Normal, healthy fear of making a mistake can be hideously distorted by turning over and over in our heads the endless possibilities of what could go wrong. While extroverts may *talk* themselves out of something, introverts *think* themselves out of it. Peter Vogt, author of *The Introvert Manifesto: Introverts Illuminated, Extraverts Enlightened*, explains it this way:

> *I think too much, analyze too much, worry too much (or so it seems). I need to act more and think less (though that doesn't mean not thinking at all). Honestly, I think I'm in my own way for the most part.*
>
> *I sometimes find myself in a situation similar to the one Indiana Jones (Harrison Ford) encountered in the movie where he was rescuing his dad (Sean Connery). Remember the part of the movie where Indiana had to take a step into, well,* air *before the bridge appeared that would take him across the gorge? That's how I feel right now about my business: I want to take the step(s), but I see a gorge and no bridge; yet the bridge won't appear unless and until I take my first step(s). I feel like I've begun that process, but it's always a work in progress.*

How many times since you started your business have you made a choice to take a step into what looks like thin air? And what happened when you did? You may have felt like you were free-falling for a while, uncertain where you were going to land. The landing might have been soft or it might have been rough and rude. In either case, you found a way to move through the discomfort and any fears that went with it. You honored your introvert preference to reflect on the experience and notice what you learned. You sat with it long enough to hear the inner wisdom. And finally, you dusted yourself off, picked yourself up, and moved on.

Fear and Overwhelm: How to Eat an Elephant

Sometimes I find myself saying the same thing over and over, to myself and to others. One particular piece of repetitive wisdom that I appreciate is this: How do you eat an elephant? One bite at a time!

It seems that so many people in my life—clients, friends, family—are always on the verge of total overwhelm. They're always in the throes of a big goal or project, and the enormity of the task casts a shadow over them that feels dark and ominous. My shadow of the past few years (actually, my dream!) was the book you're reading right now, the one I had in my head that felt called to be on paper. I started thinking of the book-shaped shadow as an elephant, and that led to fearing the beast was going to sit right down and squash the life out of me.

We know intellectually that the best way to accomplish something big is to approach it in smaller pieces. This is not only common sense, it's an advantageous approach for introverts who want to pace their energy so they have enough internal resources to finish strong. So why do we run into trouble? Why are we weighed down by the shadow rather than buoyed by the dream?

Most likely, we have some fear. We've made up internal stories about the humongous elephant that represents our goal: it's too much . . . I'll never finish it . . . What if I succeed? . . . What if I fail? . . . What if I get what I want? We're by turns motivated and deflated by the sight of that elephant's shadow.

As I mentioned, our first instinct is to break the big task down into small pieces, assuming that there's nothing else getting in our way besides the sheer size of it. It's a solid approach: Figure out what your end goal is, then figure out the first steps that need to happen to get you from where you are now to where you want to be. Focus on only one step—one bite—at a time. When you finish one thing, move on to the next.

Before You Take the First Bite

This process can be made even more effective if you spend some time in reflection first, doing that inner-wisdom gut check. Remember: As an introvert, you likely have a strong internal compass. You want to be sure it's pointing in the right direction. Before you even begin to chunk out the work, there are a few things you should do to make sure you're even pursuing the right goal.

The first thing is to reflect on your relationship to the elephant. Is it *your* elephant—in other words, is it *your* goal, or did someone dump it on you? Are you working on what *you* think you should be doing or setting a goal based on someone else's expectations? This is something for which introverts need to cultivate a sixth sense. If there's pressure to be more extroverted in the way you're choosing to move forward (and that pressure could be self-inflicted), you may be taking on goals that sound grand and noble but aren't sustainable or practical—or that simply aren't *you*.

If it's not your elephant, decide how much power you want to give it. For introverts, our energy is our most precious asset. We have to be sure we're spending it on pursuits that move us forward in the direction that's most important to us. Otherwise, we'll waste valuable energy in the push–pull between our desires and someone else's. Our own elephants are big enough without taking on ones that don't belong to us! Look at your goals: What do you have a choice about? Can you let go of goals or projects that you've only taken on to please others?

Let's assume you've determined the elephant is one of your choosing. You've named it My Bestselling Book or Revamping My Website or Leading an Association Committee or Restructuring My Fees. How do you feel when you think about being on the other side, accomplished and full? It feels great, doesn't it? Try renaming the elephant to reflect what you want to feel rather than what you want to do. Focus on your intention, which is to say, on what experience you want to have. Using this guidance, my book elephant/goal might sound like this: I feel empowered and confident as I share my unique voice with the world by writing a bestselling book.

How does that help you? By focusing on what you want to feel, you are opening yourself to possibility. You're also open to different outcomes and not attached to a specific result. It may be that your goal will take on a completely different spin over time. If you hold on rigidly to a particular outcome, you're setting yourself up for disappointment. Your elephant might evolve, and if you're too focused on a specific result appearing at a specific time, you might miss an even better result.

> *First say to yourself what you would be; and then do what*
> *you have to do.*   —Epictetus

Stepping Out of the Shadows

Even if you've confirmed your goal, broken it into smaller chunks, and set clear intentions, there are still times when you'll forget that where there is a shadow, there is also light. Here are a few additional tips for making sure the shadow of your goal doesn't leave you in total darkness.

Be Authentic

The more your goal truly arises from your authentic self, the more likely you are to be committed and take action. This is particularly important for introverts as they decide *how* to accomplish their goals.

Let's say your goal is to increase your visibility through public speaking. An extrovert might start by attending lots of events to meet people, calling up program chairs to inquire about the process of being selected, and making a video to post online. Their instinct is to reach out and start talking to people.

The introvert may start with some online research, perhaps creating a list of prospective speaking engagements. We would make sure we knew which topics we wanted to pitch before we started talking to people. Then we might start with email queries and requests to friends and colleagues for introductions.

The good news is that both approaches will work. But if the introvert does it the people-first way, he may become exhausted by trying to work out his strategy through the process of talking to others. And if the extrovert starts with research, she might become impatient and frustrated that it's taking too long. Honor your natural instincts about how you want to accomplish your goal. As Carl Jung said, "The shoe that fits one person pinches another; there is no recipe for living that suits all cases."

Know When to Just Say No

You have choices about when you say yes and no. Be mindful of how those choices affect your introvert energy; if you say yes to one thing, you may decide to balance it out by finding something of equal value to say no to. By always evaluating your energy expenditure, you'll be better able to keep everything moving forward without sacrificing your sanity.

An extrovert might feel energized by having the equivalent of a three-ring circus in his office, with lots of moving parts. But an introvert would do better to limit herself to one "ring" at a time in order to focus on what's most immediately important. Some plate spinning is OK for a while and may even give an introvert a boost (as those of us who use the adrenaline generated by procrastination as a motivational tool can attest!). Overall, however, it's helpful to watch for the tipping point when you're keeping one too many plates spinning. You want to be alert for the window of opportunity to say no to something and prevent the whole mess from crashing down.

Celebrate Your Wins

Each time you reach a milestone, celebrate it! We tend to be content with feelings of internal satisfaction when we've accomplished something, and we move on without giving it full acknowledgment. Then a few days, weeks, or months later, we're wondering why we feel so tired or like we're not making any progress.

I think it's because we've not taken time to acknowledge what we did in a meaningful—and often external—way. Celebrating externally doesn't come naturally to introverts; our instinct is to keep it private. Extroverts are more likely to reward themselves because their motivation rests in external recognition. This keeps them going and moving on to the next step, always seeing that there's a reward waiting for them. By contrast, the introvert says, "Well, I'll wait until I'm completely done before I reward myself."

Just as you broke up the goal into smaller action steps, break up the rewards, too. Cement each win by treating yourself. Hit "pause" and take time to appreciate your progress. Take an afternoon off. Visit with a friend over a long lunch. Share a quick "I finished the first part of my project!" announcement on social media (this serves the dual purpose of self-acknowledgment and receiving a few kudos from people who care about you). Enjoy a few minutes of quiet or close the door, pull the blinds, and indulge in a fifteen-second (or longer!) dance party. By acknowledging your progress, you'll replenish your spirit with positive energy, which you can then channel into taking the next bite.

Enlist Kindred Spirits

Surround yourself with people who will support you. They may be friends, colleagues, family members, a coach, mentor, or adviser. Keep connected to people who inspire, encourage, and challenge you.

An extrovert will naturally surround himself with people because that's how he works best. He'll want multiple channels of input and feed off the connections within a group. When he hits a roadblock, he has a ready group of people to call on for assistance.

An introvert will have people to turn to, but it may be a smaller group. We've learned over time that some people—even well-meaning friends who love us—can be a drain on our energy.

If we reach out for help, we're opening ourselves up to the possibility of more stress. Our friends or family may think they are being helpful, but somehow the advice they offer runs tangential or counter to our needs.

As you think about who you want to surround yourself with, choose carefully. Consider who among your colleagues has the most positive, generous spirit. You want to connect with people who are working from an attitude of abundance.

And just because someone offers to be your mentor or adviser doesn't mean you have to take her up on it. You can either be direct: "Thanks for your advice. You've made me realize how much I would benefit from working with a coach, so I've hired one." Or just avoid encouraging the relationship (say "no thanks" to a coffee date) and let it fade. It helps to remember: If you say yes to the not-an-ideal-fit person, you're saying no to having meaningful space for another, more aligned match.

Call them kindred spirits. These colleagues serve as your cheerleaders, reality checkers, and sounding boards. WhereFishSing .com's Fiona Morgan, a self-proclaimed introvert entrepreneur, finds value in talking with others when she's faced with a challenging goal. She shares, "When I identify a weak area, I look for someone I know who is really capable in this area. I observe them operating and perhaps ask them how they approach the area in their mind. It helps to have the perspective of someone who is successful at something I want to learn how to do. How they think about it is usually radically different from how I have been thinking about it."

When Morgan reaches out, she's stretching herself into a place that's not always comfortable for introverts. Our tendency is to try to figure out the challenge ourselves. But in so doing, we're denying ourselves the opportunity to gain fresh perspective. Morgan's approach—reflect on a specific challenge, find someone who has faced it and succeeded, and ask her how she thinks about it—is very introvert friendly. Most people love being asked for advice; it's flattering to them. Keep that in mind if you feel self-conscious about reaching out for help. Chances are the person will be happy to share.

Trust the Process

By focusing on the experience you want to have and making choices based on your intention, you can trust that you are moving toward your goal, even if things look different from what you anticipated. Acknowledge that the process you have chosen—being an introvert entrepreneur—is not the path of least resistance.

Here's how Christian Marie Herron of Herron Media puts it:

> *My mantra is that "Most people are not brave enough to ever start their own business. If it was easy, everyone would do it." What I have learned as an entrepreneur is that the icky feelings are part of the territory and that as long as you do something every day—write, make a call, learn a new marketing skill—these feelings will always be temporary. Over time you gain the wisdom of knowing that you are on the right path, even if you can't see clearly where you are.*

What I appreciate about Herron's perspective is that it applies to all entrepreneurs, introvert or extrovert. For the introvert, it's especially important to balance the internal processing with external action. Remind yourself that you are brave for starting a business in the first place—use that knowledge to put whatever's happening in context. You're up to big things, and few things worth doing are ever easy. Above all, keep in mind that the only way to eat an elephant—the only way to move through your fears—is one bite at a time.

> *Start by doing what's necessary; then do what's possible; and suddenly you are doing the impossible.*
> —Saint Francis of Assisi

Introvert Entrepreneur Focus

Betsy Talbot, author and founder of Married with Luggage

What was the catalyst for making the leap from being, in your own words, "like the Energizer Bunny on a dead battery" to being a world traveler and author?

Before jumping full-time into being a location-independent entrepreneur, I was a successful professional in the medical-records technology business. I loved the problem-solving aspects of my work, but the rest of the job took its toll on my energy. The part I hated the most was the constant travel to client sites and business meetings, where I was expected to socialize after hours with clients and coworkers. It left me feeling exhausted all the time, so much so it was impacting my marriage.

I eventually decided to leave the company to create my own consulting firm. Then my brother had a heart attack, and a good friend suffered an aneurysm in her thirties. That shook us awake, and my husband, Warren, and I asked ourselves, "What would we change about our lives right now if we knew we wouldn't make it to our fortieth birthdays?" We instantly knew we wanted to travel the world, and after the exhilaration of that idea wore off, the fear set in. How could we afford this? What would we do for a living? How could we give up what we'd already built?

How did you move through those fears?

My introvert instincts kicked in and provided a way forward. Rather than give in to the worry, we started doing some research and taking small steps forward. It was through that process that we had an epiphany: track our fears, questions, and actions publicly via a website. If we had these kinds of questions about a big lifestyle change, wouldn't other people contemplating big changes have the same questions?

Facing the fear gave us the best business idea of our lives.

What would you recommend to an introvert entrepreneur who is feeling anxiety about moving forward with a big idea or dream?

First and foremost, remember, it's bigger than you. Once we fully realized that the business we were creating was bigger than us, the fear dissipated. Our focus was on other people, which made it easy to slough off the smaller fears. I also realized that by making myself so vulnerable online, I was creating a support network of thousands of people who could offer encouragement. Plus, having everything documented meant that anytime I faced a new fear, I could look to my past for parallel situations. In most cases, I'd encountered—and overcome—something similar before. It was powerful to acknowledge my strengths and build on my past successes. Now, I consider fear a compass. When it crops up, I know I'm on to something.

Chapter 3

Finding Your Voice

Always do right. This will gratify some people and astonish the rest.
— Mark Twain

The Truth Will Set You Free

Any entrepreneur who expects to build a thriving business must have two things: clarity of purpose and awareness of core values. Your purpose and values serve as litmus tests for every choice you make, from what services to offer, to whom you collaborate with, to the clients you decide to work with. An integral part of the values clarification process is finding your Truth, with a capital T. As we discussed in Chapter 1, introverts can have their personal Truth obscured by well-meaning people who expect them to be different from them.

Jim Hessler, an introvert colleague and management consultant, shares that when he first took the Myers-Briggs Type Indicator, his result was almost the complete opposite type of what he actually was. He later realized that he grew up playing a role, filling a need in his family of being the logical, steady, outgoing extrovert. The people around him had so much influence over how he saw himself that it wasn't until many years later (when he was in his midforties) that he realized who others expected him to be and who he actually was were two very different things. If he had continued relying on those external projections, his life choices would be consistently out of step with his Truth. His new awareness enabled him to make more intentional choices that brought him into resonance with himself, to the benefit of both his professional and family life.

This chapter is all about establishing a solid foundation for your business so that what you build on it is, from the start, a reflection of who you are and what's most important to you. We're first going to look in more detail at what it means to find your Truth, why core values are vital and how to identify them, how to clarify your entrepreneurial purpose, and how to tap into the power of a beginner's mind.

What Is Your Truth?

This is a question that comes up frequently during coaching sessions with my clients. As we navigate through a situation or sticking point, the bottom-line question is often "what's true?" We get so caught up in FUD-generated stories about how things *should be* that we lose touch with how they *are*. Even as introverts—who typically look inward for guidance—we can spend lots of time listening to others and looking outside ourselves for the answer to our challenges. The entrepreneurial journey can be full of uncertainty, so we look for outside validation and information from people who've been there, done that.

The challenge comes when those voices end up being louder than our inner wisdom.

A certain amount of looking externally for information on how we should build a successful business is necessary; it's called *research*. Ultimately, however, once the information is gathered, it's critical to turn off the radar and let the information germinate. Combine it with what you already know without asking anyone else. By doing that, the choice—the truth—is yours alone.

Few things articulate this point more beautifully than the words of essayist and critic William Deresiewicz in a speech he gave at West Point in October 2009:[1]

> *My first thought is never my best thought. My first thought is always someone else's; it's always what I've already heard about the subject, always the conventional wisdom. It's only by concentrating, sticking to the question, being patient, letting all the parts of my mind come into play that I arrive at an original idea.*

Let's consider that for a moment: *My first thought is never my best thought.* We're always told to "go with your first instinct." And certainly there's a place for that. Sometimes that works. Other times, though—when the problem or situation is more intellectual or concrete—we need to give ourselves space for reflection. To connect the dots. To come up with an original thought. To find our Truth, with a capital T.

And that's part of what differentiates successful introvert entrepreneurs from the rest of the pack: You have taken time to have original thoughts. Rather than follow the conventional wisdom, you've put energy into coming to your own conclusions. It doesn't require conscious effort to be bolder or louder or more noticeable than anyone else. You'll become those things naturally when you give yourself space and grace to be comfortable sitting in reflection.

Even though most introverts have a powerful relationship with their inner world, spending your precious energy deep in thought, sifting through often-conflicting information can be exhausting.

Deresiewicz went on to tell us why it's so important, despite the energetic cost. He related the story of a hazing scandal at a U.S. naval base and challenged his audience to consider what they would have done if they'd been involved in such a horrible situation. The cadets wouldn't have had time to reflect, in the heat of the moment, on what they believed in. That's why it's critical to "know thyself" *before* you are confronted with a challenge to your beliefs. Your energy is well spent being proactive and determining your values so that you can summon up the courage to act on them when the time comes. As Deresiewicz noted, you don't wait until you're in the line of fire for the first time to learn to shoot your weapon.

Making choices based on your Truth is not for the faint of heart. It's not enough to simply "know thyself"; you must be willing to act on that knowledge. When you come up against a choice that goes contrary to your ideals, you must respond accordingly. You can't pretend not to know. And that takes guts. It takes courage.

It's worth taking substantial time to think about these issues when your business is still in its infancy (and even if it's into adulthood). While your core values will most likely remain consistent over time, it's also worth the time to do a check-in every once in a while, even if you've been in business for years (in fact, the longer you're in business, the more important it is to do these check-ins). Ask yourself if you are clear about where you stand on issues of importance to you and your business. You don't want to be forced into making a critical business decision based on fear or panic; you want to be able to act based on the security of your values.

Sales Success coach Tshombe Brown puts it simply: "The truth will set you free. And the truth that sets me free is that I'm Tshombe, and you're not!"

How wonderful is that? He is always secure in his truth because he is secure in himself. He knows that he has gifts that only he can give—it doesn't matter if what he's sharing has been shared a million times before, no one else can say, write, or think it like he can. Secure in that knowledge, he is *free* to express and live his truth. He is free to be the best Tshombe he possibly can be!

What's my truth, besides "I'm Beth, and you're not!"? It's a question that I ask every day. Words of truth that bubble up are *compassion*, *intention*, *grace* . . . grounded in those values, I can make choices based on what's right for me, instead of what someone else tells me I "should" be doing.

As an introvert, you know: The truth isn't out there. It's in you!

Company Culture and Values: Not Just for the Big Guys

If you're a solopreneur, chances are you've not given a lot of thought to your company culture. And if you have employees, you've probably noticed a particular culture developing, and it may or may not be intentional. In reading the enlightening corporate history of Zappos, *Delivering Happiness* by introverted CEO Tony Hsieh, I was reminded that the concept of culture is highly relevant, whether you are a company of one or one thousand. It's the place where values, truth, and purpose come together.

According to Hsieh, your culture is your brand. They are two sides of the same coin. We all recognize the importance of our brand; have we paid equal attention to our culture? Because culture and brand are on the same coin, alignment is the key to making sure your business cultivates and sustains strong value.

Value does not simply mean financial results. For purposes of this discussion, *value* is an expression of what you hold to be true and what is most important in your life and business. Values can include ideals such as adventure, agility, boldness, compassion, discipline, freedom, humor, openness, passion, resourcefulness, and trust.

When you as an introvert entrepreneur choose to intentionally create or contribute to a positive company culture, you have stepped away from being isolated or apart, and toward proactively building a community around your business based on core values. Your business choices are determined by discerning where and how your values align with your options.

Why is this important? As business owners and change agents, we're pulled in multiple directions by any number of people, each with his own agenda. That can contribute to feeling scattered and losing sight of our original vision. Energy diffused is energy lost. With a clear values "home base," we can filter out the noise that distracts us from our purpose.

Here are three steps for clarifying and aligning your values, which form the foundation for your business culture and brand:

- Identify your values.
- Align your values, choices, and actions.
- Bring the fuzzy spots into focus.

Identify Your Values

Your values are your stake in the ground, the words that represent you and what you stand for. Zappos has ten core values that permeate every level of the company and form the basis for every decision it makes. Among their values are service, change, fun, growth, teamwork, efficiency, and humility.[2]

In the spirit of sharing, here are my core values: truth, gratitude, freedom, love, contribution, curiosity, acknowledgment, and growth. *What are yours?* Take your values and put them someplace where you can see them regularly: as your desktop background, a screensaver, at the start of your business plan, posted on your website. For example, I made a Wordle (see wordle.net to make your own) out of mine, printed out the image, and put it above my desk. (A values identification exercise can be found in the Resources section of TheIntrovertEntrepreneur.com.)

Align Your Values, Choices, and Actions

Look at each area of your business:

- People: relationships with clients, customers, vendors, collaborators, advocates
- Product: goods, services, offerings
- Presence: marketing, social media, networking
- Process: finances, time management, organization

How well are your choices and actions aligned with your values in each of these areas? For instance, if you value gratitude, how is that being reflected in how you relate to each of these four core areas? Ideally, your values form the lens through which you evaluate all of your ideas and decision points. Looking through a lens of gratitude, or other values such as truth or authenticity, you can evaluate each area of your business and see whether you're in or out of focus with your values.

Bring the Fuzzy Spots into Focus

Chances are you'll determine that, by and large, you are doing a good job expressing your values through your business. You may also notice that certain values are not showing up clearly.

Here's a personal example: I value a culture of freedom. I want to experience ease and flow in all areas of my business, particularly as related to freedom around my finances and time. In reality, I often feel constricted. There's not enough time and money to do what I want to do. I've not invited freedom into my business; on occasion, I've allowed mild panic to take over. I shut down and default to scarcity mode, which means I don't have any energy to extend myself to prospects and colleagues. Noticing this misalignment is an invitation to change. It's an opportunity to become curious and clarify exactly what freedom means to me. It's a chance to define how it would feel to create more freedom through my financial- and time-management processes. Then, I can make choices and take action to support that value.

If you intentionally align your choices with your personal values, your business will naturally grow based on what's most important to you and how you've defined success. You'll also find that your days and activities have more flow and require less exertion; you will naturally have more energy to fuel your relationships. Your choices will reinforce and advance your values. The fuzzy spots you noticed are probably values that you have not fully defined for yourself. Clarity of definition and purpose will support making choices that snap everything into focus.

Our business culture is an external expression and extension of our values and involves everyone in our circle of peers, clients, and supporters. We teach others how to treat us. Through the intentional creation of a values-based company culture, we can ensure that we're sending out the right signals that help us all treat each other in accordance with our values.

Your Dent in the Universe

Let's make a dent in the universe. —Steve Jobs

Before you took the step that catapulted you over the edge of the cliff, you probably worked for someone else. You were satisfied, but also had ideas. Big ideas. It seemed that whenever you had a big idea, it wasn't enough to let it take the form of a hobby or curiosity. Your mind went immediately to the question, "How can I monetize this?" Or you began to have visions of the way your idea could change the world. Or your life.

You decided to make a dent in the universe.

Just by the very act of saying, "I'm an entrepreneur," you are demonstrating incredible initiative. You are interested in making things happen and doing it your own way. This either leads you to carving out a more entrepreneurial role within your company or going completely out on your own.

Success is connected to being clear on the size and shape of your personal dent, and then taking the initiative to make the dent happen. Here are some key questions to ask yourself as you discern your core purpose:

- What can I accomplish through this business that I can't accomplish any other way?
- How will the world (yes, the *world*) be different because of my business?
- What will this business leave me free to be and do?
- How will this business enable me to express my strengths, talents, and individuality?

Your answers add up to your purpose statement, which becomes the wings that help you soar once you've gone over the edge of the cliff. Consider how you would fill in these blanks:

Through my business, I will realize my vision of_____

_____ .

The world will be different because _____

_____ .

This business will give me the freedom to _____

_____

and to express _____

_____ .

It's pretty lofty stuff. The risks you take won't just be financial. Taking the initiative and declaring to the world, "What I have to offer is worth paying for," takes guts. There's an undeniable element of vulnerability that goes along with being an entrepreneur. This is especially true for the introvert; our internal world is rich and active, and bringing what's happening internally into the external world is a tremendous act of courage. It helps to be passionate about what you're doing, and to have a clear sense of purpose. It's also important to acknowledge yourself for the risk you're taking by stepping into the spotlight.

Your introvert strengths not only support you when you have deep internal work to do but guide you through challenging business development activities that call on your inner extrovert energy. Together, your internal and external work bring your values and purpose to life.

I Gotta Be Me

The most exhausting thing in life is being insincere.
—Anne Morrow Lindbergh

Authenticity is a word that tends to be overused, but for a reason. It reflects a way of being that encompasses many concepts at once: genuine, trustworthy, reliable. According to the *Collins English Dictionary*, it derives from the Late Latin word *authenticus*, "coming from the author," from Greek *authentikos*, from *authentēs*, "one who acts independently," from auto- + *hentēs*, a doer. For the introvert entrepreneur, there is much to love in the word *authenticity*. Living in authenticity means honoring your truth. Taking action. Coming from your inner wisdom. Being who you are, 100 percent.

This is why the expression "Fake it till you make it" makes me bristle. I've said those words myself, without really thinking about what they imply. We think that when we're about to break new ground, we have to screw up our courage and put on a brave face. We buy into the saying, "Never let them see you sweat." We believe that the antidote to our fear is to fake it. We tell ourselves that we're excited, happy, optimistic, and ready—and then we jump.

We're taught that if you actually don't feel happy, fake it. Smile, and you'll trick your brain into believing you're happy. I've tried it, and it works for a little while. For some, it might be just the answer. But at least one study contradicts that conventional wisdom.[3]

Scientists followed bus drivers over a period of time and compared the moods of those who engaged in "surface acting" (forcing a smile even when unhappy) and "deep acting" (conjuring up happiness from positive thoughts or memories).

What they found was that when forcing a smile, "the subjects' moods deteriorated and they tended to withdraw from work. Trying to suppress negative thoughts, it turns out, may have made those thoughts even more persistent." Conversely, when a subject tapped into positive memories, mood and productivity improved.

When we fake it, we're not acknowledging or honoring our truth. When we fake it, we exhaust ourselves and drain precious energy that could be spent taking our message out into the world. So what's the alternative?

First, intentionally acknowledge that the whole situation feels fake. Disingenuous. Draining. It's important not to negate the feelings that you're experiencing. If you ignore them or shove them aside, they'll come back to fight another day. Fears and doubts only grow bigger in the dark.

Second, we say *and* (not *but*), and we do what the bus drivers did: We choose to deep act. We tap into what's already inside us, what's authentic, to pull us through. This can take the form of feeling gratitude for the adventure or for learning something new. It can be curiosity, shifting from "I don't know what's going to happen" to "I wonder what will happen" (and knowing that whatever happens, you can handle it). You can conjure up memories of a big accomplishment, images of a loved one or your biggest cheerleaders.

Then, when we put on our game face, we are doing so from a place of authenticity. We've started by being transparent ("This stinks!") and moved to changing our attitude and story, drawing from people, places, and things that have heart and meaning for us. Faking it is tiring for everyone, especially the introvert. Our work is taxing enough without the added stress of putting on a mask every time we go out. We sometimes think we have to fake extroversion in order to fit in. In reality, introverts have an extroverted side that we can summon forth when we want. Being social and outgoing—relative to our introversion, not to someone else's extroversion—doesn't have to be fake.

So the next time you think to yourself, "Well, I gotta fake it till I make it," stop. Reflect. What's the positive energy within you that's waiting to come to the surface and help you through? Can you invite your natural extroversion—the part that is eager to share your passion for your business with others—out to play?

Faking is a waste of energy, and our energy is one of our most valuable assets. Spend it wisely.

Who Do You Think You Are?

Now that we've closely examined truth, values, purpose, and authenticity, there's at least one more brick to lay in the foundation of your business: authority.

It comes up in conversations about identity, especially with introverts: we frequently feel more confident when our authority lies in someone or something else. For instance, if you work for a large or prestigious company or you're marketing a product or service that has brand recognition, you feel empowered by its credibility. You are always one step removed from whatever it is that people are buying. If someone says no, you know they weren't saying no to you *personally*. You may even have a more relaxed sense of responsibility when it comes to what people think of the business. In theatrical terms, you are a member of the chorus, and you are told what to say, what to wear, and when to show up, then you do the best you can with what you've been given.

This all changes once we step out of the chorus and into the spotlight. We're exposed, and there's no one else to either credit or blame. A coaching colleague said to me, "I wish I had something other than just *me* to offer them." She was saying that she wanted her authority to be attached to something else—a model, framework, or tool—whose reputation preceded her. That's a totally natural desire, especially when you consider that earlier we defined entrepreneurial risk in terms of vulnerability.

You can apply this insecurity to almost any endeavor: Why become a massage therapist, when others are trained to do it better than me? Why coach or consult, when there are others certified in the same methods I am? Why be a photographer, when I know I'm no Ansel Adams or Annie Leibovitz? Why be an accountant or lawyer, when it feels like the marketplace has more than it needs?

The answer is that *no one else can do it like you do.* If you feel called to make a contribution in the world through your business, it's because there's a gap that only you can fill. There are people out there whom only you can serve. Your authority lies in your responsibility to make your vision come to life.

I've also found that authority comes more easily when I release attachment to being right, being the best, or having everything turn out a certain way. That might seem counterintuitive; we usually think that we feel more confidence and authority if we know exactly where we're going and we're 100 percent determined to get there at all costs. Placing our authority in certainty is greatly increasing our risk in an already risky venture. There's much more to lose if we're emotionally attached to a particular result.

When you release attachment, you allow yourself to be more open to opportunities. You are better able to tap into your introvert strengths of listening, reflection, and curiosity—to explore beyond the norm. Introverts prefer going deep rather than wide, focused rather than scattered. If you combine that depth with openness, you are setting a bigger stage for yourself. Maybe even all the world!

Releasing attachment has a magical side effect: Our fear of failure diminishes. Even the word *failure* starts to take on new meaning and release its power over us.

> *We must be willing to let go of the life we have planned, so*
> *as to have the life that is waiting for us.*
>
> —Joseph Campbell

Reframing Risk

We're going to wrap up this chapter by revisiting the word *risk*, because it's a close cousin of *failure*, and being able to embrace both is key to your success. Usually when we hear the word *risk*, we think of it as something to avoid. But consider the definition of *entrepreneur* on Dictionary.com: "a person who organizes or manages any enterprise, usually with considerable initiative and risk." You are *expected* to take risks—in other words, to make mistakes. To fail. It's part of the job description.

Inventor and introvert Thomas Edison offered this wisdom: "Of the 200 light bulbs that didn't work, every failure told me something that I was able to incorporate into the next attempt."

Edison probably came to that conclusion after a lot of teeth gnashing and frustration, especially in the beginning. Lucky for us, his realization can save us a lot of time and energy. He basically grants us permission to fail. In fact, he's reminding us that it's highly probable that what we're trying won't work out at all!

It may be beneficial to reframe *risk* as *research*. It's information gathering. It's trying something out and knowing that you'll learn something from it that will be useful the next time. Whatever it is that you're doing, it's not an end in itself—it's one step on the journey.

To fully appreciate this, we have to approach our risks with a beginner's mind.

Here's how I learned my biggest lesson in risk, failure, and the beginner's mind. When I decided to enroll in a coach-training program, it took a while for a certain reality to fully sink in: I was going back to school. While it wasn't school in the traditional sense, it pushed the same buttons. The biggest button, lit up and flashing wildly, was the "good student" button.

It was within this context that I was introduced to the concept of a beginner's mind. Your beginner's mind approaches each experience with an open mind, free of assumptions about what you should know, what you don't know, what you're good at, and what you're challenged by. It releases judgment about what's good or bad, right or wrong, success or failure. It lets go of the labels (even the label of introvert, if that's been a source of negativity or feelings of less than) and embraces what shows up.

For me, the power of adopting a beginner's mind was obvious in each of the three-day classroom sessions I had during the eighteen months of training. The first classroom day, my coaching would be relaxed and in the moment. I didn't know what I was doing, so instead of feeling anxiety, I felt more curiosity and willingness to take risks. With each subsequent day, as my mind was filled with experiences, self-judgment, and new information, I found myself coaching more from my head and less from my heart.

We have the power to reframe risk into something that works for us, not against us. We entrepreneurs have to have a fairly high tolerance for risk . . . it's not a question of *if* we will take risks, but *when*. If we don't take risks, we'll stagnate. We'll actually *lose* confidence. We won't learn how to pick ourselves back up when we inevitably fall. But here's the good news: When we take risks, we learn that we don't have to have all of the answers or get it perfect. We have the choice, at any moment, to come from a beginner's mind, live from our core values, and see ourselves and our businesses with open eyes, open minds, open hearts.

Introvert Entrepreneur Focus

Brad Feld, author, blogger, and venture capitalist at Foundry Group

Most entrepreneurs begin their journey being driven by something that's important to them, that they deeply believe in. It's easy to lose our way, though, as the business grows and pressure mounts. Why is building a business that's in alignment with our values important, especially for introverts?

It's something I see within the technology industry, entrepreneurship, and venture capital all the time: People create a persona for themselves and for their companies, and then their actions don't match it. So you have this huge disconnect between words and action.

That's not just toxic for the business and for what you're trying to accomplish; it's also toxic for individuals. There's the dissonance of trying to portray a certain way of being and then having your way of *actually* being inconsistent with that over a long period of time; [it] is emotionally . . . incredibly hard. It creates lots of broken relationships and internal inconsistencies that are exhausting.

Entrepreneurship requires a lot of trial and error, often in a very public arena. How would you advise introverts to handle that particular kind of stress in a healthy way?

There are going to be situations as an introvert where you find yourself working on something or trying something publicly that you're not very good at. I don't care whether it's a business or sports or music or whatever, it will be uncomfortable. It will be draining. It doesn't mean that you shouldn't exercise those muscles. You just recognize that exercising those muscles is exhausting. And when you use up your energy you have to recharge, turn around, and go through your energy again.

What beliefs do you hold most dear, that influence your perspective on life and business?

I believe in the wonderful line "Life is a process of continual oxidation." We're always in this process of dying, so you have this finite experience where really you're kind of always working toward the end.

Another belief is, "We're all just bags of chemicals." Each person's a different bag of chemicals, and do you want to end your life a bag of chemicals or a bag of broken glass? Every time somebody hugs you they get cut because of how sharp and miserable you are, or do you want to be recognized that you're a bag of chemicals and let that continue to evolve?

So for me, experiencing the journey, the good and the bad, knowing that it has finality at the end, is so much more important than the individual things that I accomplish along the way.

Chapter 4

You Must Be Present to Win

Networking for
the Introvert Entrepreneur

This chapter is the longest in the book, and with good reason. First, it's an absolutely essential activity. Second, whenever I've asked introverts what they find most challenging about being in business for themselves, they inevitably mention networking, usually in the same breath as sales activities. Here's what people have shared with me over the years:

> "I don't like walking into a noisy, crowded room where I don't know anyone."

> "Small talk is so challenging. I always feel like I go on and on, and the other person is just looking around the room, trying to escape."

> "I feel pressure to sell when I go to a networking event. Otherwise, why go?"

"Networking wears me out, especially those happy-hour events that have no structure."

"I'm good at networking with my peers, people who are in the same type of business I'm in. I'm not so good at networking with potential clients or customers."

"Networking has gotten easier for me over the years, but I still feel like it's a necessary evil rather than something I enjoy."

"I hate networking!"

Do you hear echoes of your own experiences in their words?

Just as we reframed fear in Chapter 2, here we're going to reframe networking in such a way that you feel more comfortable inviting more of it into your business development activities. After all, your business—regardless of whether it's Internet, service, or product based—depends on you pounding the pavement, knocking on doors, seeing and being seen. But before we get into the details, let's look at why networking is such a hot topic for introvert entrepreneurs.

Networking: A Hell of Our Own Making?

An introvert's natural habitat is one of quiet and solitude or with smaller groups of people. We feel most comfortable and relaxed in an environment that allows space to think, to have meaningful conversations, and to control how much stimulation is coming our way. For most introverts, networking represents the complete opposite of our natural habitat. Networking events are often noisy, random, and awkward . . . at least, they can feel that way if we're nervous or uncertain how to make ourselves comfortable in an overwhelming environment.

What are the biggest obstacles that get in the way of introvert entrepreneurs being effective networkers? The answer is the stories and beliefs we have about networking: that it's about selling, and that it's full of awkward "What do I do now?" moments, meeting lots of people, uncomfortable small talk, and judgmental strangers.

Of course, not every networking event is the introvert's definition of hell. There are times when the hell is of our own making because we decide that it's going to be awful or stressful. We might concoct untrue stories in our heads about being an introvert and therefore being socially awkward, shy, unmemorable, or otherwise inadequate when it comes to small talk. The event itself might be pleasant and (dare I say it) even fun, but we close ourselves down to those possibilities because we've decided in advance that networking is to be endured, not enjoyed.

Successful networking depends on creating new stories and beliefs that increase our capacity for this important business development activity. The experience will always be what we make of it. This chapter will show you how to reframe networking from something exhausting and unnerving to something productive and energizing.

What I Learned from Getting Nudged Out of the Car by My Introverted Husband

My husband, Andy, taught me one of the most important lessons I'll ever learn about networking. It was while I was in my first job, for a very small nonprofit dance company in Milwaukee. My recently obtained master's degree had prepared me for the technical tasks that had to be done: marketing, fund-raising, negotiating contracts, and managing a budget. But I was not prepared for the people side of things and, specifically, for networking.

Andy, also an introvert, had the very unintroverted job of public relations director at a large arts nonprofit organization. He had to know how to connect with a wide range of people, from donors to musicians to media. That meant that networking and going to lots of events was important to his work, and because I was married to him, that meant it was important to me, too.

One rainy winter night, he had to make an appearance at an event held by a colleague's agency to celebrate an award they had received. The venue was a bar and would, I was sure, be full of people talking too loudly and standing too closely together. So I sat in the car and whined to Andy, "I don't want to go in. I don't know anyone there. It's going to be loud, and I'm too tired." I'm sure my voice made it clear that if he made me get out of that car, I was going to make him miserable.

His reply got me out of the car that night and still helps me get out of the car even today. He said, "It's true, you might not know anyone in there. But you might be surprised. And each time you go to one of these events, you'll see one or two or three more people that you know. One day, you'll walk into the room and know half the crowd. That takes time, and you have to start showing up *now* if that's ever going to happen."

Even sixteen years later, I remember and treasure his simple advice. I appreciate it even more now, knowing Andy better and understanding how it's sometimes an effort for him to work up the energy and enthusiasm for yet one more meet and greet. But you would never know it seeing him in action. Some of the things my introvert spouse does that make him successful:

- He knows how to connect with people in a way that doesn't completely exhaust him.
- He focuses on one person at a time.
- He steps off to the side of the crowd so he can hear better.
- He asks lots of questions so that the spotlight is on the other person.

Watching him, it's clear that being comfortable with networking is not something you have to be born with; it's something you can cultivate.

If you have to network anyway, you might as well find a way to make it less painful and more profitable.

"Eighty Percent of Success Is Showing Up"

When I first heard the Woody Allen quote that heads this section, I thought of it in the traditional sense. "Showing up" meant going to the meeting, the party, the networking luncheon, even when I didn't feel like it. There were days when I definitely felt like my introvert energy was pulling at me to stay in my office, behind the computer, so I could type instead of talk. On those days, networking was a "should" and "have to" activity. And even if I showed up physically, I would be in another place mentally (usually imagining my happy place—someplace quiet and alone!).

Those early weeks of opening my business involved lots of blissful alone time as I worked on my website and materials and strategy. But it wasn't long before I realized that showing up was going to be the foundation of my marketing strategy. There was no way I was going to be able to build a successful business just by sitting behind my computer and sending emails. Because my traditional view of networking was not only energetically draining but also time-consuming, I was going to have to employ different strategies to make connections with people beyond gritting my teeth and physically showing up. It was the only way I could both grow my business and protect my introvert energy.

Who Are You?

Before we get to those strategies, however, pull out your notes from the company and culture section of Chapter 3. If you formulate the intention that you're going to show up more often in more places, ask yourself: Who am I showing up as? Think about your personal presence and what attracts clients and customers to you. As a coach, I show up with a coaching presence: attentive, curious, and nonjudgmental, which I mix with my personal introverted style of being generally calm and listening more than I talk. What is your presence? Are you playful? High energy? Intense? Curious? Reassuring? Provocative? And how does that presence align with what your current and potential clients expect of you? Showing up as your most genuine you, with the energy and passion you bring to your work, goes deeper than simply walking the talk. It's the edge that allows you, the introvert, to stand out in an extroverted crowd.

The Fine Art of Showing Up, Introvert-Style

By deciding to experiment and expand my rather strict definition of networking, I discovered four distinct strategies that work with the strengths of introvert entrepreneurs. They are showing up *to* people, *through* people, *for* people, and *for yourself.* You can apply these strategies anytime, anywhere.

Showing Up *to* People

This is perhaps the most obvious of the showing up opportunities. It means to be completely present—physically, emotionally, mentally—to others. You give the situation your full attention and energy.

Remember that no matter where you are showing up, you are representing your business. Are you showing up in a way that reflects your values and attitudes about success and client service? What's your intention when you enter a room of people?

For me, the question is, "What do I have to offer here?" rather than "What will I get out of this?" This mindset allows me to receive ideas and opportunities that might otherwise have been filtered out. It also opens up more referral possibilities.

Sometimes nervousness or anxiety can kick in, and we become the opposite of introverted: We chatter and say things we wouldn't normally say, especially if we place an expectation on ourselves that we're going to get business at a networking event. Matt Youngquist of Career Horizons offers this piece of advice to introvert entrepreneurs who have a tendency to put pressure on themselves to be assertive with their sales agenda: "One key mistake many people make when it comes to networking is to ask too much, too soon, of a new acquaintance." If the intention of your networking is to prospect for new clients, it's poor form to directly ask a new acquaintance for personal referrals. Youngquist goes on to say, "In most cases, such an 'ask' is going to be too aggressive before a sufficient amount of mutual trust has been established."

Youngquist's advice relieves us of the (often self-imposed) pressure to sell and reminds us that it's more important to be clear on who we want to connect with: "What an enterprising entrepreneur *can* do is clearly describe the types of individuals they're most hoping to meet (e.g., venture capitalists, social media experts, people working in a given industry, etc.) and leave it in the hands of the new acquaintance to *volunteer* some potential referrals, if they're comfortable doing so."

In-person networking is the most energetically demanding strategy for the typical introvert. It requires a projection of energy that is much more physical and active than, for example, when we're connecting with people online. It's also potentially more draining because we are absorbing and reflecting other people's energy.

Therefore, we need to thoughtfully plan and prepare ourselves for events. This might mean you schedule only one event in a day or week. If you have more than one in a day, you can choose to leave plenty of buffer time between events so that you're not rushing from one to another. You can also practice the buddy system, enlisting a friend or colleague to attend with you and thereby relieving some of the anxiety of not knowing anyone.

How do you use your social media networks? Social media is one of the introvert entrepreneur's best tools, allowing us to pace our interaction and be especially thoughtful about how we present ourselves. Think about how you can show up authentically through your blog, website, email, Facebook, LinkedIn, Twitter, and all of the other ways you are connected to friends, colleagues, and prospects. Here's an example of how this has worked for me: I received an email from a friend I'd not spoken to in a while. She remarked that she'd "always been tempted by my invitations" and had decided to take action and contact me about coaching. Because I'd taken care to use my online presence as an extension of how I physically show up as coach, this friend saw me sharing wins and opportunities as an invitation to learn more, not as a sales pitch.

Showing Up *Through* People

During the year I trained to become a coach, I was out of town for one of my weekend classes. When I returned, I hadn't been home ten minutes before my husband, Andy, told me that he'd reconnected with a childhood friend in Minnesota who was interested in becoming a coaching client. Two things led to it: First, Andy's sister knew what I was doing and told this friend. Then the friend talked to Andy, and he also mentioned it. Without me needing to be present, two people promoted my services, and a client was born.

This is one of the best ways to expand your reach while still preserving your energy. Find those people who are your biggest cheerleaders and advocates. They could be family members, friends, teachers, mentors, and professional colleagues. Reach out intentionally, in person if you can, or via Skype, VoIP, or phone if distance is a challenge.

At the most basic level, you'll want to learn more about each other's businesses and needs so you can extend your reach to more people. This process is about cultivating a group of mutual champions. Each person in the relationship is actively seeking opportunities to promote the other. In order to do that, you need to know the basics of each other's services, exchange a small stack of business cards, and make it easy to talk about each other (this requires being confident with your elevator pitch, which we'll cover in a few more pages). Share what you're both looking for in a client or project.

One of my mutual champions is a personal organizer who works with women going through life transitions. If I encounter someone who would be an ideal client, I'm confidently able to refer her to my colleague. As she crosses paths with entrepreneurs who are introverts and want to build sustainable businesses, she mentions my name.

The goal is to create a true win-win situation. And in time, the relationship may extend beyond referrals. You may find that you have enough synergy with your mutual champion that it evolves into a formal collaboration or partnership down the road.

Remember your former satisfied customers and clients in this equation, and stay in touch as your business grows and changes. Their testimonials, success stories, and referrals are the ultimate in showing up through others. It's easiest to ask for these things while the client or customer is still with you because he's probably feeling positive about you and your offerings. It takes more energy for anyone, but especially the introvert, to reach out after the relationship is over, because we can experience that anxiety of bothering someone or wondering if he's going to remember our working relationship fondly—or remember it at all.

You can avoid the extra work after the fact by identifying where in the cycle of your client or customer relationship it makes sense to ask for a referral or testimonial. For service-based businesses, where a client is with you over a period of time (such as coaches, consultants, massage therapists, trainers, financial and legal services), incorporate a process check or other touch-base opportunity at a set point in the relationship. Ask how she's finding the service, if she has any suggestions, and would she recommend you to a friend. Go an extra step and ask, "How can I make it easy for you to tell others about my services?" A certificate for a free session or consultation to pass along? A few business cards? Some brochures? A blog or e-newsletter to share online? Most people enjoy being asked for their opinion and sharing resources with others, so capture the opportunity while that person is still a client.

If your business is product based, you could create an in-store or online customer satisfaction survey and include the survey URL (with an incentive, such as a discount on a future purchase) on their receipt. More personal, high-touch purchases could be followed up with a quick phone call or email, asking about the customer's experience and suggesting that they share their experience with others (assuming it was positive!). Make this easy for yourself by writing a short phone script or an email template so that you can make the follow-up as efficient as possible. Turn it into a routine; there's no need to reinvent the wheel every time you solicit feedback. Keep it short, simple, and direct. And try setting aside a block of time dedicated to this type of follow-up. It's often more productive and less energetically draining to make five calls in a row and be done with it rather than spread them out through the day or week and have them nick away at your time and energy.

Showing Up *for* People

As a successful professional, you recognize that showing up for other people creates community and shared prosperity. It extends your network in unexpected ways. And you have the potential to learn something new from everyone you meet.

One of the ways we show up for others is when we attend a workshop or event they are hosting. When I hosted my first tele-class, several other coaches participated in support of my new endeavor. I can't tell you how wonderful that felt! I've since tried to return the favor to my colleagues as my time and energy allow. By engaging with other entrepreneurs in this way, you're establishing stronger relationships and making it easier to reach out for assistance when you need it. It's also an easy way for the introvert to make meaningful connections with only minimal energetic output; this is especially true when the events are virtual or over the phone.

Other ways to show up in support of others include:

- Send a handwritten thank-you note when someone gives you a referral, testimonial, or useful resource.

- Write a comment on a colleague's blog, reciprocate a link, retweet, or offer a thoughtful reply on a social media post.
- Take a moment to write a compliment or provide an endorsement on someone's social media profile.
- If the person is an author, write a book review, whether it's on Amazon or Goodreads, or as a blog post.

Joining an entrepreneur network was one of the best things I did when I started my business. The group had a wonderful philosophy of collaboration, not competition. Their consciously cultivated sense of "we're all in this together" helped me notice when I was being competitive rather than collaborative.

As a result, I came to realize that my competitive attitude arose from a scarcity mentality. I was seeing things through a lens that told me there was only so much to go around: finite resources, clients, projects, and opportunities. I noticed it most when I'd go to an event and be surrounded by more experienced coaches. It was challenging to look at them and think, "Someday, that will be me." Instead, I thought, "I'm not at their level." It was déjà vu all over again, because I had those same thoughts when I started graduate school: I perceived my peers as more talented musicians than me from day one. This led to a slow downward spiral of self-sabotage as I kept telling myself stories about not belonging or being good enough. While I personally grew by leaps and bounds during those years and choose to view that period with no regrets, I sometimes wonder how the outcome might have been different had I not been coming from a scarcity mentality.

A "me versus them" mindset also emerged when I saw those who were more outgoing as having an advantage. Because I was judging my energy against those who showed up more extroverted than me, I thought my piece of the pie was even smaller. If it's not caught quickly, that mindset can lead to isolation and fear, two deal breakers for any introvert entrepreneur.

Lastly, there's an element to showing up for others that involves success by association. The more you're around the people who have done the things you want to do—write a book, host success-ful workshops, give keynote speeches—the more normalized such activities become. Your support of their success means you have increased opportunities to learn from them and view them as role models or mentors. And if you've reached the success that others crave? Be there for people who want to be encouraged and reminded that the journey of a thousand miles begins with a single step.

Showing Up *for Yourself*

"This above all: To thine own self be true." Doesn't that sound like the introvert's modus operandi? These words of Shakespeare's Polonius in *Hamlet* are simple enough, yet the implications are profound.

Tending to your own needs first is among the most important pieces of showing up that you can do. With entrepreneurship, the line between the personal and professional is thin and fuzzy and sometimes nonexistent. If we're not taking care of ourselves and taking time to restore our energy, we're not going to be fully avail-able for our businesses.

So often, I hear someone say, "I just don't have time for myself. It's impossible to make that happen." My empathetic but firm re-sponse: You can always make time. It's not about finding the time. It's about deciding that it's a priority. You're letting your feelings of guilt or a fear of neglecting others override your natural instinct to take time for yourself.

Deciding to show up for yourself can take several forms: It may mean scheduling your days in a way that reflects your natural rhythm and energy. Perhaps it's taking time for a nap, or being selective about whether you meet someone in person or schedule a phone call, or saying no to the fourth evening event in the same week. Practice giving yourself what you need with small things, such as staying home instead of going to the movies, so you can read or exercise.

Then when it's time to make decisions about the bigger things (such as choosing to lease an office instead of working from home), you'll be more comfortable with it and less likely to feel pangs of guilt or second-guessing. Think about what values are most important to you and how you are turning those values into actions. Staying true to your core and practicing meaningful self-care means you will have more energy for all of the other showing up you want to do.

Now that we've explored different ways of showing up in support of you, your goals, and your business, let's look at three additional considerations for successful networking:

- How to use your introvert energy to your advantage
- Expanding your definition of networking to include multiple approaches
- Practical steps you can take before, during, and after networking to both protect and leverage your introvert energy

Use Your Introvert Energy to Your Advantage

Introverts seldom realize they have an advantage when it comes to networking situations. This is primarily because they think of it as an outgoing, social activity that has the high potential to lead to a mental meltdown. To compensate, introverts are sometimes tempted to try to be an extrovert in these more "out there" functions.

Instead, I encourage people to tap into the part of them that is naturally extroverted and to meld it with their introverted need to listen, observe, and internalize. By understanding what natural strengths you bring to the process, you can transform what could be a highly stressful experience into one that provides you with vital connections and information. Here are some traits that come so naturally to most introverts, we might not realize that they are networking gold.

Listening

Introverts often like to listen more than we like to talk. That's one of the reasons we get the quiet or shy label, because we're not as vocal as our extroverted counterparts. So rather than force yourself to talk more, relax into listening more. Allow the other person to carry the conversation. Listen fully, without thinking ahead to what you're going to say when he stops talking. Trust that when there's an opening in the conversation, you'll know what to say or ask. It's usually a simple matter of picking up on a word or phrase he said, or reflecting back to the speaker with a statement such as "It sounds like you . . . ," which shows you heard what he said and that you were interested and want to hear more.

Curiosity

Because of the aforementioned preference for listening over talking, introverts often have a fairly fine-tuned curiosity. We'd rather ask questions and shine the light on someone other than ourselves. To make the most of this, have a few stock questions ready in advance that you can pull out at opportune times. For example, you can ask, "Have you been to one of these events before?" "What do you enjoy most about these gatherings?" "Have you heard this speaker before?" "How did you get started in your business?" "What goals or opportunities are you most excited about this year?" And one of my favorite questions, which takes a little courage but is worth the risk, "What's making you happy today?"

Think about questions that are positive, easy, and friendly without being too personal. More questions will come to you as you talk with someone. And here's another key to being more comfortable in networking conversations: Be prepared to answer these same questions yourself. Chances are the person you're talking to will turn the tables on your questions and say, "What about you?" Avoid the deer-in-the-headlights moment by knowing how you'd respond to your own questions.

Observation

Look around the room and more closely at the person you're talking to. There are dozens of clues in your environment that light the way toward easier and more natural conversation. This can range from talking about the space itself (if you happen to be in an interesting venue) to the person's tie, scarf, or jewelry.

Notice little things that provide insights into the other person's interests or personality. Sometimes we're given a gift: She's wearing a necklace with a tennis racket pendent, or he's sporting a Rotary Club pin. These are obvious openings for questions. Don't worry if you're not a tennis player or a Rotarian. People who wear their interests on their sleeve (literally!) are often happy to chat about their involvement and answer questions. Other times, the lead-in may not be so obvious. That's when you can look for anything about the event or gathering that's unusual or worthy of comment.

Another way to use your powers of observation is to notice if there are other people who look like they're new to the group, uncomfortable, unable to break into group conversations, or just hanging back and watching. They may be shy or not sure how to approach the situation.

Imagine if that person were you. What would you want someone to say to you? How would you want to be brought into the conversation? If someone takes the time and trouble to come to an event where he's expected to mingle and reach out to people, it's safe to say that giving him a helping hand would be appreciated. Consider how you'd feel in the same situation, and graciously invite the person into conversation. He will probably be relieved and grateful for the lifeline you've tossed him, and you'll feel more relaxed because you've helped there be one less anxious person in the room.

Quality over Quantity

Building a networking strategy on the premise of *the more, the merrier* doesn't necessarily resonate with the introvert entrepreneur approach. Most anything written about networking says the same thing: It's about making meaningful connections, not collecting a stack of business cards that you can stuff in a drawer at the end of the day. However, there are still people who consider networking a numbers game. They believe that the more people you meet, the more you increase your chances of meeting *the* person who will lead to a breakthrough of some kind.

Perhaps there is some truth to that; if you cast your net a bit wider, you are more likely to encounter someone who will impact your life or business. But let that guide what *types* of events you choose to attend, not how many. Introverts have a tendency to enjoy having a few relationships of depth and substance rather than many superficial ones that scatter our attention.

Knowing that, choose your associations based on their fit with your values, goals, and ideal market. If you want to join a networking group, visit several before you decide which one to commit to. Talk to members to find out what they like most about the group and what value they're experiencing. If you feel aligned with a group's vitality and purpose, it won't matter if there are five, fifty, or five hundred people in the group; that alignment will boost your energy rather than drain it. Even so, consider going to two highly strategic events each month rather than wearing yourself out by going to a dozen general networking activities. When you get there, focus on one-on-one conversations and making solid connections with two or three people. You'll preserve your energy, feel more positive about the experience, and walk away with more promising leads.

Some Enchanted Networking

Guy Kawasaki, who happens to be an introvert entrepreneur, wrote a book called *Enchantment* that's, well, enchanting! He defines enchantment as "filling others with great delight." Consider that and look back on what we just covered as introvert strengths: listening, curiosity, observation, quality over quantity. There are few things more enchanting than someone who is embodying those four strengths.

Put yourself in the position of someone who is benefiting from an intentionally enchanting person. That person is actively, deeply listening to what you have to say. He's genuinely curious and asking you easy questions. He's noticing things that make this experience much more interesting. And he's just talking to you, not letting his attention wander to the one hundred other people in the room; he seems sincerely invested in your conversation and making a true connection.

Imagine! If someone embodied those strengths, those enchanting behaviors, you'd think he were a networking superstar, wouldn't you? That's what you, as an introvert entrepreneur, have the potential to do, every time you meet someone new.

Everyday Networking Opportunities for Introverts

So far we've mainly been talking about formal networking events that you attend for the explicit purpose of networking with your peers and prospects. Now let's expand our definition of networking to include any activity that puts you in front of people with the possibility of talking about your business or learning about others. In this new definition, every time you step out your front door, there's a networking opportunity just waiting to happen. Don't let this definition give you more excuses to stay at home; it's simply a reminder that sometimes the most powerful connections happen when we least expect them.

Entrepreneurs who love their business are always ready to share their passion, even if the setting is not one in which they'd expect to talk about their work. Speaking from your heart and your passion helps you move through the more introverted tendency to keep to ourselves and not initiate conversation. With practice, you will start to see small, everyday opportunities for sharing your message in casual conversation.

Career coach Matt Youngquist notes that people's mistaken assumptions often blind them to opportunities for making good business contacts. "A huge roadblock in some people's networking efforts relates to their (mistaken) belief that they can reliably predict who can help them—and who can't—in reaching their goals. I routinely meet people who only network with people in their own industry, for example, or who marginalize the potential usefulness of neighbors, church acquaintances, gym buddies, hobby group members, and other categories of people they have in their social circles."

It's easy to fall into the habit of networking only with peers or friends; it's comfortable and safe. And it limits the number of people who can potentially support you. As the saying goes, "It's often the last key that opens the lock." Sometimes it's the person you least expect who will lead you to a new opportunity.

As you look to expand your circle of acquaintances, it's helpful to be clear about what types of networking situations you enjoy and are most productive for you. Most introverts don't like happy hour or unstructured networking events. Consider that networking can happen anywhere, such as at a lecture, book signing, workshop, presentation, or retreat. I like workshops, because it's a mix of like-minded people and potential clients and collaborators. There's also a focus, so there's a natural topic for conversation.

Here's a short list of ways we can meet others who may end up being pivotal to our success:

- Attend professional meetings, conferences, or conventions
- Participate in workshops, lectures, or book discussions
- Get involved with political or religious groups
- Visit with other parents during your child's extracurricular activities
- Volunteer for causes you care about in your community
- Form or join a meet-up group (try meetup.com)

- Visit with other people who share your hobbies or interests
- Talk with your neighbors
- Strike up a conversation with someone while waiting at the doctor's office, in the checkout line, or while you're getting your hair cut
- Search out friends (current as well as former) on Facebook and Twitter
- Connect with current, former, and potential colleagues on LinkedIn
- Share an interesting article or resource with a colleague
- Reconnect with former teachers and classmates
- Meet someone for an informational interview

What else could you add to this list? Consider your daily routine and places where you have casual opportunities to engage with people. Opportunities for making connections are crossing your path every day.

Where You Are Now, Where You Want to Be

In addition to where you network, consider who might be there when you show up. Seek networking opportunities that put you in contact with people who are doing what you want to do rather than always being around people who are in the same position you are (for example, other inexperienced or new entrepreneurs, people who provide the same products or services, or people who are struggling). Be intentional about expanding your circle to include those who are a few steps ahead of you, or who have already accomplished what you want to accomplish (writing a book, having a six- or seven-figure business, working with a national clientele, setting up multiple locations, etc.).

There is value in networking with other entrepreneurs who are in the same business development phase as you, especially in the early years; in these groups, you are reassured that you are not alone in your anxieties, insecurities, and questions. And you can commiserate and brainstorm together about possible solutions.

However, make sure you don't get stuck there, networking only with people who are like you. It's important to show up in places where your ideal clients or customers hang out. Notice when you're spending more time with your peers than with your prospects, and find ways to stretch into new networking territory (strategically, of course!).

Effective Networking, Introvert-Style

Now that we've looked at the big picture and expanded our definition of networking, let's turn to actionable tips and tricks that will help you reframe networking forever. We're going to examine the art of networking through an introvert entrepreneur lens, looking at what you can do to both protect and project your energy before, during, and after the event.

Before the Event

> *To be prepared is half the victory.*
> —Miguel de Cervantes

In general, introverts like to prepare. It takes less energy to walk into a room prepared than it does to wing it. Respect that desire to be prepared by taking steps to gather information and do your homework before the event starts.

First and foremost, whether or not you're good at networking starts in your head. It's a frame of mind. Depending on your previous experiences, you may have the idea that you're not good at small talk, you don't like talking to strangers, and you won't know what to say when you do end up talking to them. You may also have a general I-don't-like-networking attitude. One way or another, all of these attitudes will come through in how you present yourself, even if you don't tell a soul how uncomfortable you are. This is why it's important to reframe your beliefs about networking.

Reframing something does not mean denying it. Instead, *reframing means putting a different perspective on the thought so that you can work from love instead of fear.* This is something you'll hear from me time and again in this book because approaching our work from fear rather than love is at the root of so many of our challenges. When we come from a place of love, there's no room left for fear to have any power.

When we're trying to shift how we think about something, it helps to acknowledge through our affirmations that we are at the beginning of our journey. If we feel insecure yet tell ourselves, "I'm a rock star networker! I love meeting strangers!" our introvert brain is going to reject these thoughts as lies. The most effective affirmations use words and phrases that acknowledge that change is a process. Saying "I am beginning" and "I am becoming" (a tip I picked up from motivational speaker Andy Dooley) is much easier for your brain to believe. Here are a few affirmations that have worked for me and my clients:

"By relaxing and letting my personality shine, I am becoming more comfortable with talking to new people."

"I welcome the opportunity to learn more about others while sharing the wonderful gifts that I have to offer."

"I am ready for the new connections that come when I show up from a place of curiosity, gratitude, and authenticity."

"I am beginning to appreciate my quiet energy and how it helps me connect with others."

I invite you to use these or make up your own. The important thing is that you find a way to remind yourself of the unique and fabulous strengths you bring to the table. One of my favorite affirmations comes from the book *Feel the Fear and Do It Anyway* by Susan Jeffers. She tells us to remember, "I can handle whatever happens." One of our biggest fears is that we won't be able to handle or deal with something. In truth, we can handle anything. And you can handle any networking situation!

Here are additional ways you can prepare yourself in advance for a positive networking experience.

Set an Intention

What do you want to learn? What experience do you want to have? Do you want to make a particular connection with someone? Do you want to practice talking comfortably about your business? Think of intentions that are focused, reasonable, and stretch your skillset. Consider these examples: I want to meet three new people and learn about their business. I want to feel calm and centered during the event. I want to practice asking questions rather than talking only about me. I intend to greet everyone with a smile and a confident handshake. I intend to learn how I can help or provide resources to two other people.

"Pre-Care" Yourself

If you need to prepare by making sure you have some alone time, a nap, or some exercise, make those activities a priority. Do what you know builds up your energy. Leave yourself time in your schedule before and after the event to recharge and relax. Think twice before agreeing to carpool with someone or meet for coffee before or after the event. It may be that those interactions serve as a warm-up, or priming the pump, before you have to walk into a roomful of strangers. It may also be that you need that time to be spent quietly to clear your mind and shore up your energy. Say yes to those types of invitations only if you really mean it. All of this planning is a way of taking care of yourself—or "pre-caring"—in advance.

Do a Little Online Stalking, Um, I Mean, Research

We have a treasure trove of mobile information at our fingertips, often right in our purse or pocket. I highly recommend tapping into it in advance of any event or meeting you're attending. If there's someone you're interested in meeting, visit her website, check out her social media profiles, and even read a few blog posts or articles to get a stronger sense of who she is. Use web-based information to build a bridge between online and off-line.

Have a Short Introduction Prepared

For this bit of networking preparation, I have found inspiration in Simon Sinek's book, *Start with Why: How Great Leaders Inspire Everyone to Take Action*. He discovered that there's a communication pattern that leads to greatness, which he calls "the Golden Circle." He posits that the reason we have trouble connecting with and influencing people is because we take too long to get to the heart of why we do what we do. We focus on telling people *what* we do, which is often followed by sharing *how* we do it. And in most cases, we never get to the *why* at all.

According to Sinek, "People don't buy what you do, they buy why you do it." I find this viewpoint particularly resonant for introverts because we are generally more focused on the inner world of ideas and images (whereas extroverts tend to spend more time in the outer world of people and things). Every business was sparked by an idea (a *why*), yet we sometimes lose our connection with that spark when we get caught up in the *how* and *what*—the outward manifestations—of the business. The Golden Circle framework helps us describe what we do (starting with the *why*, then moving to *how* and *what*) and serves to take the focus off of us as individuals and even off of the goods and services. Instead, it rekindles our relationship with our inspired idea and initial passion.

Sinek proposes that we consider three important questions, asked and answered in this order:

Why do you do what you do? "I believe . . ." Start off by sharing why you do what you do. Focus on what inspires you and what gives you the energy to keep on going when others may have quit. So you're a coach, designer, massage therapist, butcher, baker, candlestick maker . . . so what? What do you offer that makes you more worthy of my dollar than the other person doing exactly the same thing? What do you most believe in? Why does your business matter? For example, here's one version of my *why*: "I believe in the magic that happens when people trust themselves."

How do you do it? "The way I do it is . . ." This might be your proprietary process or value proposition that differentiates your product or service from everyone else. It's more tangible than your why. It might be quantifiable or qualifiable, and it also describes the action you take to make your *why* come to life. "The way I help people increase trust in themselves is by empowering them with information about their energetic type."

What is "it"? "I make this happen by offering . . ." The *what* of your statement is the result of your *why* and your *how*. It is the products and services that people purchase from you. This is the most straightforward part of your introduction, yet it is more meaningful when it comes last rather than first. You've piqued someone's curiosity with your first two statements, so this is where you make it concrete: "I make this happen through individual coaching with introverts who want to amplify their natural strengths."

The process of identifying your *why-how-what* is not as easy as it may seem. Notice that I introduced my example *why* with the words "one version." There are multiple reasons why I started my business, and I'm willing to play around with different phrases depending on my audience or the platform. Give yourself the same space. This may not be comfortable at first; most of us introverts like to know precisely what we're going to say before we say it. Practice your *why* at larger events where you're meeting new people. Because here's a helpful little secret: Chances are no one is going to remember your exact introduction next time they see you (if you ever meet again at all). Also, it's likely the person you're talking to is too busy thinking about what she's going to say when you stop talking! Sometimes we think we'll cause market confusion if we vary our introduction from event to event. The truth is that unless you have an extremely memorable, sticky statement, they'll remember only the type of business you have.

Allow that knowledge to free you up from needing to have the perfect words before you start networking. The language you use will probably evolve as your business evolves. Over time, you will develop different lead-in words or find more succinct ways to make your point. You'll settle into an introduction that feels comfortable, and you might find that you actually enjoy the process of introducing yourself and your business to someone new.

Honor your desire to project confidence and to shake off any nerves by practicing your introduction until it feels completely natural and unrehearsed. Val Nelson says, "Connect from the heart. Rehearsed words and pitches usually land on deaf ears. Just connect. Be yourself. Find common ground even if it's not relevant to your offerings. You both have a new puppy? Then talk about that. When they're feeling it, they'll naturally ask what you do and stay engaged in the conversation."

No matter how you structure your short introduction or how you respond to the "What do you do?" question, keep the emphasis on your *why*. This strategy is perfect for the introvert entrepreneur because it keeps the focus on our offer rather than on us as individuals. What's the benefit you offer or the problem you solve? Here's a great example I heard at an event a few years ago: "I connect people with resources to causes they care about." His profession? A fund-raiser for a nonprofit. He put the emphasis on his contribution rather than his job title.

Being able to answer those three questions shouldn't take more than twenty seconds or so. It's not a rundown of your entire business plan. It's a simple way to structure a teaser that lets listeners decide if they want more. And rehearsing will help you be relaxed and flexible when it's time to deliver. Know who you're talking to and practice customizing your answer to fit the audience.

Another benefit to these questions? They shine the light on how well you've niched your business. It's worth really drilling down to craft a statement that reflects your motivation, personality, and niche in a way that unquestionably differentiates you from everyone else.

During the Event

All men's gains are the fruit of venturing.   —Herodotus

The networking event itself doesn't have to be exhausting. There are a variety of ways you can take care of introvert energy and still make meaningful connections with people.

The first—and perhaps most important—thing to remember is to relax and breathe. Allow yourself space to notice tension in your body or if you're holding your breath or doing too much shallow breathing. Lower your shoulders, roll your head, shake your hands, yawn, smile. I find putting my palms over my eyes for a few seconds, with my fingers resting lightly on my forehead, brings me a sense of peace and calm. You can do this casually when no one notices or realizes what you're doing, or excuse yourself and use the restroom for a quick relax-and-breathe break.

The next tip might seem obvious: Wear comfortable clothing—nothing too tight, short, big, small, or itchy. It's challenging to relax and be fully present when you're constantly wishing you could sit down and take off your once-comfortable, now-painful shoes for a few minutes.

Here are more ways you can tap into your introvert strengths during the event:

Start slowly; don't immediately throw yourself into the thick of things. It's not necessary to jump right in, shaking lots of hands (you're not running for president). Sip a beverage and watch the group. Watch others as they interact for clues about how people are working the room. Seek out someone you know to help you warm up to the room and the event. Ask your friend to introduce you to someone she knows, which is easier than a cold introduction.

I learned a great trick from Arden Clise, president of Clise Etiquette: "When you're making an introduction, offer a small piece of information to each person that will facilitate conversation. For instance, if Joe is a mountain biker and Sally just finished summiting Mt. Rainier, share those tidbits and let their mutual love of the outdoors ease them into conversation." You may not always know these types of details about each person, but if you do, find a way to work them into your introductions. As an introvert, you'll be glad the informative introduction you made between two people takes off easily without any additional input needed from you.

Take on the mental role of host. Set an intention that you will focus on making others comfortable and welcome by smiling, asking questions, and drawing out folks who look uncomfortable (perhaps fellow introverts . . . ?). Don't spend lots of energy trying to be dazzling or charming—it will happen naturally—and instead focus on being fully present, curious, and sincere. Own your energy, inside and out.

The question mark is your best friend. The best conversationalists are those who have genuine curiosity about other people. Ask questions about the other person's work and interests. Use those observation skills again to look for clues for conversation, such as an unusual business name. Notice what seems to light the other person up—it may be his family, recent travels, talking about his business—and ask questions that encourage him to talk. You can certainly talk about yourself; there's a strong chance that your conversation partner will turn the tables on you and say, "I just returned from South America. Where have you traveled lately?" You can decide what you're comfortable sharing in the moment because you've prepared in advance.

Focus on talking to one person at a time. You may find yourself as part of a small group, but even then, focus on the person talking or asking the question. Make eye contact with everyone, but don't feel like you have to scan the group the whole time. Use your introvert gifts of making one-on-one connections to your advantage. It can be very flattering to the person you're talking to if you are truly focusing on her.

Paula Swenson, artist and founder of Creative Spirals, offers, "Concentrate one hundred percent on the person in front of you and ask questions, then really listen to the answers. So few people listen; doing so will make you stand out from the crowd. Plus, it is much easier as an introvert to listen than to talk."

Be yourself. Don't think you have to be really outgoing and extroverted to be an effective networker. Show up with your natural curiosity, sense of humor, and ability to listen. During the event, preserve your sanity by taking breaks as you need to by stopping into the restroom or lounge, slipping out for a quick walk around the block or down the hall.

Decide when you've had enough. Share your energy while it feels good, and give yourself permission to leave when you've had enough. Say good-bye to the people you want to connect with later. Don't feel like you need an elaborate excuse to leave. There's no rule that says you have to be the one to turn out the lights.

After the Event

The greatest oak was once a little nut that held its ground.
—Anonymous

Where do most people fail to make the most of networking events? It's not how they show up at the event itself; it's how they show up—or don't show up—afterward. They continue to be little nuts, not realizing that with some cultivation, they could grow into mighty oaks.

For many introvert entrepreneurs, even following up with self-identified leads can be challenging. These are leads for which the person fills out an offer sheet, asking to be contacted. Or maybe the person handed you her business card and said she'd like to learn more. A lead couldn't get much warmer, yet we're often diffident about reaching out to them. What's up with that?

Chances are it's those pesky FUDs rearing their ugly heads again in the form of negative self-talk. We may think to ourselves, "Oh, she just said that to be nice," or "I don't know, he didn't seem like he'd be my ideal client." We come up with excuses and procrastinate—and meanwhile, someone else is following up with that same lead and making progress on the relationship. I've heard from various sources that the majority of sales happen after at least eight contact points through email, phone, and mail. Eight! Other sources cite between five and twenty-plus touches are needed before a sale is made. And the bad news for prospects who need their services is that most entrepreneurs—especially phone-adverse introvert entrepreneurs—stop after just one or two attempts.

The sad truth is that most people don't follow up, even when a prospect opens the door for us. You will stand out in the crowd—and flex your introvert relationship-building muscles—if you follow up within twenty-four to forty-eight hours of meeting someone. You'll also demonstrate that you care about their business if you practice patience and persistence when it comes to cultivating the relationship. I've seen opportunities take several months to come to fruition, not the days or weeks that I wish they would. Remember, you and your prospect have different timelines, and they are almost never operating according to yours (which is invariably much faster!).

It's important to develop a sense of when your communications are starting to be heard, and when they're falling on deaf ears. You can waste a lot of your introvert energy on people who are flat-out not interested but keep stringing you along. If you sense that's happening, give them an opening to cut the cord. Be direct and say, "I want to explore this opportunity further, and I sense that the timing may not be right for you or that I might not have what you need. If that's the case, just let me know. I only want to continue the conversation if it's going to be beneficial to you."

Here are a few more tips for reluctant networkers on following up:

Send each person you spoke with for more than a few minutes a short email or snail mail note. (Helpful hint: These days, a handwritten note makes a more lasting impression.) Reference something you discussed, how he or she can reach you, and leave the door open for a future connection (such as "I'd appreciate the opportunity to talk in more detail about your business"). Don't say you'll be in touch again if you won't, and don't make a sales pitch at this point in the conversation. Keep the focus on the other person.

Finish what you started. If you offered an introduction or referenced an article or book, follow through by making the needed calls or emails as soon as possible, preferably within a forty-eight-hour window. The longer it takes you to complete these tasks, the more difficult it becomes and the more excuses you will generate.

File the info someplace where you can use it. After the event, write on the back of each person's business card the date, event, what you spoke about, and any follow-up actions. Keep a file (electronic or paper) of contacts you can reference as you meet others. Being able to connect others ("You two should know each other") is a valuable networking skill. People also remember fondly the person who connected them to a person, book, or other resource. Each time they come in contact with that resource, they're likely to think of you. And how wonderful is that for us introvert entrepreneurs!

The Mother of All Networking Events: The Professional Conference

Close your eyes and think back to the last big conference or symposium you attended. What do you see? Hear? Feel? Chances are your recollections are very similar to my own: You see hundreds of strangers. Your schedule is full of back-to-back meetings in large, impersonal rooms. There may be a noisy exhibition hall, with vendors smiling behind dishes of chocolate and vying to get your attention. In the actual sessions themselves, you have to endure small talk and icebreakers. And if that weren't enough, the last session doesn't mean your day is over because you feel obligated to attend the "optional" happy hours and city tours.

For most introverts, any one of these situations in a day would be draining. All of them at once? Totally exhausting!

Yet, it's usually these things—and more—that we encounter every time we go to a large event or conference.

In spite of all this, believe it or not, I actually love going to conferences. Even though the logistics drain me, I enjoy hearing interesting speakers; getting takeaway information in the form of handouts, worksheets, and resources; and being challenged to think in new ways. I always figure that if I come away with at least one inspiring idea, paradigm shift, or meaningful connection, it was worth the stress and expenditure of energy.

But when I think back to various events I've attended, even the ones I was extremely interested in, I had to force myself to go. Just anticipating the event made me preemptively exhausted. Thank goodness for the conferences that provided a minute-by-minute schedule; I could sit with it each morning and do a mental dress rehearsal, plotting my entrances and exits.

The challenge is that most large events seem to subscribe to the notion that we have to be together every second of the day and cram every minute with activity to get our money's worth. If you want to slip away for some quiet time, you are inevitably going to miss a keynote, a session, or a meal—all undesirable options when you've paid good money to be there.

Conference Stressors and Their Antidotes

Patty K. is a fellow introvert entrepreneur who asked me to team up with her to do a survey of other introverts about their experience at large events. Patty initiated the project after coming back from an event where she talked to several people who said they were overwhelmed and had to drag themselves there, "because I know it'll be good for me," as nearly everyone put it. Patty's hunch was that there were lots of introverts who wanted to attend events and wanted to have a good experience, but a large conference's plethora of offerings was just downright anti-introvert!

One highlight from the survey was a list of the biggest stresses introverts experienced at large events:

- Unstructured networking
- Little to no opportunity for meaningful connections
- Not enough places/opportunities to get away from crowds
- Pressure to attend social activities before or after—and in addition to—the regular schedule

When asked what effect these stresses had on their event experience, one respondent wrote, "When I take breaks or leave early, I feel like I'm missing out, even though doing so is crucial to my sanity." Another said, "I usually love [these events] and spend a lot of time with lots of new people (although no parties and annoying exuberance please!), but I'm knackered the week after."

Since the occasional large event is part of every entrepreneur's experience, it's good to have a few survival strategies to help you make the most of the situation and lessen that knackered feeling:

Give yourself a break. Nothing says you have to be present every minute of every event. Look at the agenda and decide in advance when, if needed, you can go back to your room or go for a walk. Often you can get the handouts, a recording, or notes from a colleague afterward. The event planners give you a schedule and act like it's do or die, but you have a choice to follow it or not. The alternative is ending the day feeling like you've been run over by a Mack truck . . . which doesn't exactly support having a positive, energizing experience.

Focus on making others feel welcome. Smile, ask questions, and draw out those who look uncomfortable. Think of a few stock questions in advance: "What's the best presentation you've been to so far?" "What ideas are you most excited to implement once this is over?" or "What did you think of the lunch keynote?" These are especially useful questions for breaking the ice during the rubber-chicken dinner session.

Plan for your comfort. A few things we know for certain: Room temperatures fluctuate, and food quality is often a toss-up. It's easier to stay present and focused on your learning when you're not distracted by physical discomfort. Consider the advice from this survey respondent: "Planning *really* helps, for instance, bringing a bag with layered clothes, drinks, and snacks to events with a packed schedule."

Quit while you're ahead. Don't pressure yourself if you feel you'd rather take a pass on the social extras and obligations that come with being at an event, including (but not limited to) happy hours, early breakfast meetings, and going out with the gang for dinner. While you might feel out of the loop temporarily because you missed hearing the story about the time your boss caught a fish "this big," chances are you'll appreciate your choice to recharge alone much more. Learn to say a firm "No thanks," and without excuses or being defensive, take care of yourself.

Until that day when planners intentionally make events more introvert friendly (which I'm guessing more than a few extroverts would appreciate as well), we'll just have to take matters into our own hands and do what we can to take care of ourselves. In fact, that wisdom applies to much of the introvert entrepreneurial journey.

Introvert Entrepreneur Focus

Bryan Janeczko, founder of Wicked Start,
NuKitchen, and StartOut

Most introverts hear the word *networking* and think of working a room at an event. You have a different perspective; how do you define *networking*?

I define *networking* as managing a select group of contacts for a specific business outcome, whether that's establishing new contacts or maintaining existing ones. In my case, I might "network" to gain more user traction or find investors interested in promoting entrepreneurship. It's about engaging others in my "why" and expanding opportunities. By approaching networking this way, I can leverage my introvert energy. I'm more inclined to listen, take time for myself, and focus on one person at a time. Typically, when I'm out in a public setting and networking, I tend to *appear* much more extroverted. However, I do focus and find that making one or two deeper connections is more valuable than a dozen superficial connections.

You're a fan of Simon Sinek's *Start with Why*. How has knowing your *why* made you a more effective networker?

My entrepreneurial mission—obsession, actually—is to help people reach higher ground with easy, step-by-step processes. In every business I've owned, it's about serving the customer. This common thread is my personal "why," which is my reason for doing what I do. By starting with an authentic expression of who I am and what I believe, I'm able to translate my "why" into business opportunities. Even more than that, I'm willing to go that extra mile to achieve success.

I have the perfect example of how it's worked for me: During NuKitchen's early days, we were looking for ways to gain more visibility. We thought a celebrity connection would do the trick. My cofounder and I put our heads together, and it didn't take long to figure out that Sarah Jessica Parker was our ideal celebrity connection.

We all know someone who knows someone. I happened to be at a party where I met Broadway director and choreographer Jerry Mitchell. After a little small talk about his work, it was clear that he knew anyone connected to Broadway, including Matthew Broderick, Parker's husband and star of *The Producers*. Another acquaintance, Kristin Chenoweth, was also a friend of Matthew's, so I had two connections and an increased chance of reaching Sarah Jessica Parker.

Ultimately, Broderick was asked to try our service for a month, and he said yes. After a month, he continued for another month, so we took the bold step of asking if his wife would try it. Within a day, his assistant got back to me and said yes. After she received the food for a month, both Parker and Broderick agreed to let us use their names to promote our product. So within three months of us figuring what—and who—we needed, she was on board! Our sales more than doubled, and I'm convinced that it led to other amazing opportunities for the business as well.

What are some other ways introverts can make networking work for their business?

There are three things that you can do to be a more productive networker and, by extension, be seen as an expert in your area. First, use social media to identify your select group of contacts. Be active on discussion groups, post questions and answers on LinkedIn, and engage with others through introductions and recommendations. Identify people to meet in person, and make the initial contact online. Second, suspend judgment about who will be helpful and who won't. Every time I made a snap judgment about someone, I have been proven wrong. Sometimes the very person I was writing off turned out to be a savior, providing a new client or maybe an investment opportunity. And finally, reach for the stars. Remember, famous people might be famous, but they're first and foremost *people*. You might be surprised at how receptive they are to being approached. If you think getting a celebrity's endorsement or business would benefit your business, put the intention out there. Tap into the six (and often fewer) degrees of separation you have to anyone in the world.

Chapter 5

"But I'm Not a Salesperson!"

I might be going out on a limb by saying this, but my guess is that most of you reading this book didn't wake up one morning, spring out of bed, and declare, "I want to go into sales!" (*Yeah, that's not happenin'.*) Yet, I've met lots of introverts who woke up one day and declared "I'm going into business for myself!"

Did they know that they were essentially saying the same thing?

Why It Feels Like You Spend 90 Percent of Your Time *on* Your Biz and 10 Percent *in* Your Biz

There's a common frustration shared by entrepreneurs during that first year in business: "I didn't know I was going to have to be selling and marketing so much. I'm doing more networking than I am doing what I got into business to do!" In other words, you're tapping heavily into your reservoir of extrovert energy to get your business off the ground. It may feel like you're spending about 90 percent of your time on marketing, networking, and sales and only around 10 percent actually delivering the services or products that make up your business. This may, in fact, be your reality for at least the first year, if not longer.

There are many reasons we stick with it, despite our urge on some mornings to stay under the covers and not come out until retirement. We stick with it because during the "entrepreneurial honeymoon" period, our pure passion and enthusiasm carries us through and gets us out of bed. Our inner extrovert has been naturally amplified, and selling comes more easily because we're excited about our new venture.

Over time, however, all of the risk, initiative, and need for profit weighs on us. We spend oodles of time marketing and promoting and networking and doing *everything except* what we went into business to do. We start to wonder if we're cut out to be an entrepreneur, because the sales side exhausts us.

If you're reading this book, you may be tired, but ready to be energized, introvert-style. There's a refrain that we'll be revisiting over and over in these pages: Being a successful introvert entrepreneur requires that we be intentional about our energy. We have to create processes and approaches that support our personality and style. When it comes to marketing and sales, one size does *not* fit all.

The Niche: Putting Your Stake in the Ground

When I researched coach-training programs, I saw message after message that encouraged me to "train to be a life coach!" I picked a program that resonated with me and started my journey in earnest. As I progressed through my training, I heard another cacophony of voices saying, "But don't call yourself a life coach." What? Train to be one, but don't call yourself one? At first it didn't make sense. It was actually very frustrating.

I discovered later the problem with meeting someone new and introducing myself as, "Hi, I'm Beth, and I'm a life coach": It's not specific enough. It's more of a professional category and less of a description of what I provide for someone else, and it doesn't even come close to being a reflection of my *why*. It lumps me in with thousands of other life coaches who claim to be able to serve anyone and coach them on anything.

As I explored both through conversation and online research what it would mean to define a niche, I was surprised by how much resistance many entrepreneurs had to the idea of narrowing their market. Some embraced it, while others talked about it as if it were a last resort. "I don't want to turn anyone away" was the go-to reason for why someone hadn't declared a niche. "I don't want to focus down too far" was another.

In truth, these well-intentioned reasons have the potential to undermine even your very best marketing efforts and can lead to the following:

Confusion. The market doesn't know who you are or what solutions you can provide for them. Remember everyone's favorite radio station? It's WIIFM—What's in it for me? If it's not clear who you serve, and to what end, your messages will all sound like static. People have two different reactions to white noise: They ignore it or they get annoyed by it. If your message is clear and focused, static will disappear for the people meant to hear it.

Exhaustion. If your message borders on white noise, you are going to wear yourself out trying to reach everyone. Your energy for marketing is one of your most precious—and often scarce—resources. For the introvert, it requires expanding your capacity zone (more in Chapter 9), day in and day out. Without a niche, your ideal client is anyone with a pulse, which means you are almost forced to spread yourself micro-thin in order to reach as many people as possible. It's like getting up every day on a small stage with a weak bullhorn and trying to shout your way through the crowds in the market . . . oh, and your small stage is surrounded by hundreds of similar small stages, all trying to reach the same people. It's a recipe for energy drain on a massive scale.

Building a business that's OK but never fabulous. Many businesses bump along without a clear market. They believe in diversification, and see defining a focus as putting all of their eggs in one basket. This might be a successful formula for some. But what often happens is that the business becomes a "jack-of-all-trades, master of none." This goes contrary to the introvert's desire for mastery, to go deep rather than broad. We're looking for the both/and solution: being able to serve a narrow market with diverse offerings.

Determining a niche—or a target market, ideal customer, or the center of your brand bull's-eye—is one of the most important things an introvert entrepreneur can do to break away from being an average, blend-in business and enter the realm of great. A well-defined niche allows you to focus your message on your ideal clients, rather than on the masses, thereby saving you time, money, and energy.

What My Niche Journey Might Tell You About Your Niche Journey

Be distinct, or be extinct. —Tom Peters

As I started out as a professional coach, it was quickly apparent that a niche was something that was going to haunt and taunt me. I understood the wisdom of having a specific and clear focus. Finding what that focus was, however, was a bumpier road than I expected. It wasn't that I was afraid to close the door and say no to a particular audience; instead, I was interested in so many things that I would reject any idea that didn't give space and usefulness to all of my curiosity.

In the beginning, I did lots of research. I alternated between drowning in overwhelm and flying with inspiration. Sometimes I thought I'd landed on a focus, and I'd try it on for size. I started calling such experiences my "niche du jour" because they were fresh at sunrise and gone by sunset.

One day, in late 2009, I sat down and wrote out profiles for my current clients. I included gender, age, profession, reasons for coming to coaching, and what themes had emerged as we worked together. I found lots of personality traits that overlapped, but no common demographic or marketing segment. Frustration came and went over the next few months. I began to wonder if I was experiencing a new entrepreneurial phenomenon: NDD, or niche deficit disorder.

So, I gave up. I stopped trying to force it. I finally realized that I was not going to choose my niche; it was going to choose me. I decided to see who I attracted when I showed up authentically, open, and curious.

My epiphany came six months later during a business development workshop that gave validity to looking at psychographics (which include attitudes; values; and activity, interest, opinion [AIO] variables) as factors in determining one's market. I pulled up my client profiles, and guess what? The answer had been there all along, in my own words, written right next to each client's profile. In the margin of each description, I'd written "introvert." It was a true Eureka! moment. I was ready to read that word and fully appreciate its promise and possibility.

That was my niche journey. Yours will be different, and only you can write it. However, reflecting on mine led me to extrapolate three simple ideas that may make your journey smoother:

Trust yourself and the process. Most introverts I know love to do research. We love to be prepared and have all the facts before we make a decision. Therefore, in the journey to identifying your ideal client or customer, you will probably want to do some research to get ideas and context. Here's the challenge for you: Let that research inform, not define, your choice. Trust your instincts. When you feel excitement about a particular type of client and dread about another, notice it. Don't be swayed by advice that all the money is in XYZ industry or clients. And don't get too wrapped up in how many other people are serving a similar niche. (Not very many? Perhaps that signals market opportunity. Lots of people? Clearly there's demand!) If the idea (or reality) of working with those clients leaves you feeling like you swallowed a brick, trust that feeling and move on. You'll do your best work—and be rewarded for it and energized by it—when you're working with people who light you up.

Just like no one person can meet all of your needs, neither can your niche. I'm eternally grateful to my friend and fellow introvert entrepreneur Lynn Baldwin-Rhoades for her powerful question to me: Are you looking for a single niche to fill all of your needs? Indeed, I had been! We often think that if we could just find a way to incorporate everything and everyone we love into one niche, we'd be golden. What we forget is that choosing a specific market doesn't preclude exploring and enjoying other possibilities on the side. Think of your niche as the stone dropping into the water, creating a powerful presence; the ripples are related rings of expansion and curiosity. Each ripple encompasses a new possible market, but you're focusing your time, energy, and resources on the center.

Working from fear-based thoughts constricts ease and flow. Where's the love? Remember what I said a moment ago about not being swayed by advice that tells you to choose a particular clientele because that's where the money is? If you choose a niche or market based purely on financial considerations, there's a good chance you'll be making that choice based on fear: fear that your ideal market won't pay, fear of breaking from the mainstream, fear that following your heart will mean sacrifice. Also notice if your fear is rooted in the social aspect of your chosen niche. Are you concerned that it will require you to do more networking and socializing than you enjoy? Do you worry that your niche will put you in contact with people whose energy might overwhelm you?

Those are certainly factors to consider, but notice if you see them as negatives because of fear or because they mean you'll have to exert more energy. We tend to find energy for the things we love, even if we're concerned they'll deplete us. Fear, however, is more challenging—but not impossible—to power through. Consider if you have the energy both to deal with the fear of the thing and the thing itself.

On the other hand, choosing from love means that you are aligned with your values and your heart. Opportunities will flow. You will show up authentically and with passion. Marketing will be done with relative ease. You can work from intention (how you want to feel) and invitation (rather than "I need clients!"), which is much more effective and fun than forcing a square peg into a round hole.

The wise words of Kurt Cobain speak to this point: "Wanting to be someone else is a waste of the person you are."

Once I untied myself from the stranglehold the niche question had on me, I felt powerful. Free. Aligned. I felt like the person I am, and the person I'm meant to be. If you give yourself the space and grace to experience the same, you'll be well on your way to being a sustainable and successful introvert entrepreneur. Be open to outcome, not attached. Be intentional and invite the niche in, and see what shows up.

The Old Story About Being in Sales and Self-Promoting

Part of the problem that introvert entrepreneurs encounter is that we carry around an old story about what it means to be doing sales.

Much of the messaging that we see out in the marketplace has a slick, salesy feel or a bait-and-switch approach or, worse yet, it's not fully transparent or promises unbelievable results. We see so many people employing highly aggressive tactics that we start to wonder, What am I missing? Do these techniques actually work? Do I have to sound like *that* to attract clients and customers?

Approaches like this must work for some people because they continue to use them. These tactics may be annoying, but perhaps there is something about them—their directness, consistency, customer-focused message—that we can adapt and modify to an introvert style. *Tip:* Any time you find something or someone annoying, pay attention: There may be a vital lesson to be learned. One of my mentors calls this "finding the homeopathic dose" of whatever is annoying me. It often points to an area for growth. For example, if you find yourself triggered by someone's in-your-face approach, there's an aspect of it that you actually admire. The very directness that annoys you might be exactly what you need more of yourself! The trick is making it your own rather than imitating.

One of the negative self-talk loops I've heard over the years from introvert entrepreneurs—and thought myself—is that "I'm bothering people" when I promote my business. It doesn't matter if they filled out a feedback form or requested information; when it's time for me to reach out to potential clients, I'm worried that I'm going to catch them off guard or that they're not going to remember me. Or worse, that they checked the "Please contact me, I'd like more information" box just to be nice. I make up a story about the person, and that causes me to be hesitant or even apologetic about following up with him.

It's important to realize that these stories are just that—stories! They're not based in fact, and if I decide on the person's behalf that I'm forgettable, not worth her time, or just a nuisance, how do you think I'm going to come across when I actually do pick up the phone to call her? When you start to recognize your own negative self-talk, it becomes easier to discern what's fact and what's fiction, where you're making assumptions, and how you might be sabotaging the follow-up simply by projecting feelings onto your prospect that just aren't there.

Why Introverts Are Natural Salespeople

Whenever there's an old story that's recognized as being no longer useful, there's an opportunity for a new story to emerge. Chapter 1 detailed the types of stories that introverts grow up with, such as being a loner, shy, or not good with people. It's natural that those stories—which in time can become beliefs if they're not refuted— might translate into an introvert believing that he's not cut out for sales. After all, the typical image of a salesperson is someone who is outgoing, friendly, bold, enthusiastic. An introvert may be all of those things, but she may not wear those feelings on her sleeve. She may express herself in a more reserved way that isn't always understood or acknowledged by those around her.

Introverts have numerous natural strengths that enable them to be genuine in what would normally be considered a "sales" situation, such as talking with a prospect or making a direct pitch to a customer. I call these strengths "superpowers," in part because they are often hidden from view yet supply us with the energy to leap tall buildings in a single bound (and land very quietly, of course). In order to take advantage of your superpowers, there are two important housekeeping items to attend to first:

> **Get over yourself.** Your superpowers will be depleted if you get in your own way by overthinking and being *too*

inward. While an introvert's preference is to put the focus on the other person, we can become self-absorbed when we're feeling anxious. Worry is one of the biggest culprits. We get up into our heads and the hamster wheel starts to turn with questions like, What am I going to say? What will they think of me? What if I say the wrong thing? What if they don't like me? In the end, it helps to remember that it's not about you; it's about your prospect, her problem, and your solution.

Get outside yourself. You are a conduit for the message, not the message itself. Once you've gotten over yourself, it's much easier to shift the spotlight onto the other person and his problems. This perspective also comes in handy if the prospect says no. Again, it's not you who's being rejected. There's something in your message that isn't resonating or that person wasn't your ideal client. Either way, by developing some objectivity you can step outside yourself and extract valuable lessons for the future.

Five Steps to Transforming Your Superpowers into Sales

> *Let the world know you as you are, not as you think you should be, because sooner or later, if you are posing, you will forget the pose, and then where are you?*
>
> —Fanny Brice

Once we recognize and own our introvert strengths, we can start to put them into action on behalf of our bottom line. Consider adopting the following steps as a way to reprogram the way you approach the sales process as an introvert:

5. **Reframe how you think about sales.** Get the image of the sleazy car salesman out of your head. The activity is "business development," and you are an educator. You are sharing information that benefits others. When you educate, you're offering the who, what, when, where, and why of your services or products, and you're opening the door for someone to decide what to do with that information. If you don't educate him, you're not opening the door. As an introvert, I love this point—being a teacher takes the focus off of me and puts it on my message and on the listener.

6. **Remember why people say no.** People say no because you are either offering the wrong information or you're talking to the wrong market. Makes sense, doesn't it? It makes me think of a great saying that every entrepreneur should have tacked up on the wall: "A confused mind always says no." And your prospects will be confused—and say no— if you are offering wrong information or talking to the wrong people. Often, both are wrong because they are too broad. We want to be able to serve everyone, which means that our message has to speak to everyone, which is impossible! If you describe your ideal clients or customers as "they have a pulse," consider this next point . . .

7. **Rehearse your why-how-what.** We explored this concept in Chapter 4. One of the biggest challenges I've seen among introvert entrepreneurs is that we're often clear on our value proposition in our heads but stumble when someone asks us directly. Being able to answer your why-how-what questions with ease and clarity is one of the

biggest gifts you will give yourself and your business. Once you have figured out your answers to these questions, practice saying them out loud. It may not feel natural at first, but if you don't, all the words that are perfect in your head will tumble out in a nervous twitter when you're put on the spot.

Let's revisit these specific questions:

> *Why do you do what you do?* As author Simon Sinek puts it, "People don't buy what you do, they buy why you do it."[1] Start out by sharing what motivates you.

> *How do you do it?* This adds action to your *why*. It includes your unique attributes that distinguish you from your peers.

> *What is it?* Finally, you reveal what it is you do. Remember, you don't have to explain every service or product in this short introduction. Your goal is to capture someone's interest and provoke curiosity.

8. **Resist the temptation to rush the process.** Give space for the other person to hear your message, think about it, and take the initiative. It's a dance, and the right partner will follow your lead. Yes, there is a time and place for polite persistence. It's helpful to remember, though, that our introvert tolerance for silence (either during or after a conversation with a prospect) can be low when we're in scarcity mode. If you've offered the right information to the right market, giving the process ample space will create an aura of confidence, security, and trust. Come from abundance and practice patience.

9. **Repeat.** Business development, sales, and education are ongoing, day-in and day-out processes. You will constantly be discovering new things about yourself and your business. As you receive feedback from your ideal clients, you'll be adjusting your strategy and message. Everything you've been working on—reframing your story about sales, remembering why people say yes or no, rehearsing your value proposition, and resisting the temptation to rush things—will strengthen over time and become second nature. As you learn to trust yourself and your value, others will reward you with their trust and business.

Content Is King: How Working *on* and *in* Your Business Can Be the Same Thing

> *If you don't know where you are going, any road will take you there.* —Cheshire Cat, *Alice in Wonderland*

Business development is not something set apart from your passion that keeps you from doing what you love. Rather, it *enables* you to do what you love. For me, being able to reframe *sales* to "education" makes a big difference in how I approach sharing my message. My sales calls are really prospect or discovery calls. I don't like thinking of the process in terms of "getting clients." Instead, my mission is broader and more prospect focused. I'm inviting people to partner with me in changing the way the world sees introversion. I trust that the partnership will bring abundance if I'm providing the right information to the right market while creating clear value.

Offering strategically crafted content to your prospects is one of the most powerful ways you can create value. It doesn't matter what service or product your business is centered around; your prospects need information to make an educated decision. A creative approach to content can make the difference between a prospect holding you at arm's length and seeing you as the go-to person for your product or service.

The other benefit for the introvert entrepreneur is that having outstanding content is a way to keep the focus on the message rather than on you. You can express yourself in ways that showcase you at your best. You're offering high value to a range of people, many times without even having to interact directly with them (thereby saving your energy for the times when it's required to interact).

How do you get started creating content for your business? When you're first starting out, there's a certain amount of spaghetti strategy that we all engage in: You're throwing things up against the wall and seeing what sticks. You're probably churning out a lot of content. Much—if not all—of that content is probably free. And you get good feedback and encouragement . . . just not the sales.

This stage is the thrashing stage, where you're getting just enough positive feedback that you think if you just do more, faster, better, bigger, people will convert to clients. For most introverts, this would be exhausting. It's a lot of energy out but not a lot coming back at you. What's missing is strategy and intention behind your content.

Julie Fleming, author of *The Reluctant Rainmaker: A Guide for Lawyers Who Hate Selling*, was the first person who introduced me to the Cycle of Failure. Here's how she describes it: "You're looking at the bills sitting on your desk, and you say, 'I need clients. I need clients now.' You start doing all of the activities that you've ever heard of that might lead to getting clients. It feels really frantic because you're trying to do all of this different stuff all at once. And then what happens is absolutely nothing. Then you experience a crisis of confidence." The self-talk that accompanies that crisis only serves to escalate the thrashing. You may start to believe you can't attract the clients or customers that you need and that you never will.

The Cycle of Success may start off with a similar "I need more business" urgency, but instead of thrashing, you plan. You reflect on your strengths, what's worked in the past, where your prospects are hanging out, and the best way to strategically reach them. Then you execute that plan. As Fleming puts it, "You're building external indications that you actually know what you're doing." As you strengthen relationships, you start to turn those relationships into business. You fine-tune the cycle as you learn what works and what doesn't, and you do it from a place of confidence.

It's important to recognize which cycle you're in. The Cycle of Success produces forward, focused movement (even if progress is slow). The Cycle of Failure does not, probably because it produces confusing messages. I want to repeat this very important point: *A confused mind always says no.* That confused mind might say, "Great work, loved the newsletter!" but it doesn't take the time to connect the dots that you have scattered all over the page.

How Do I Create a Strategy for My Content?

If we're going to connect those dots into a clear picture, it's important to have a framework that helps you clarify your content strategy. There are many different ways you can approach building that framework, including mind mapping, creating an editorial calendar, or keeping an online or off-line idea file. No matter what technique you use, it's useful to anchor your strategy in the tried-and-true maxim: Someone needs to know, like, and trust you before he will invest any time, money, or energy in you or your business.

We say "know, like, and trust" all the time, without digging in and examining exactly what that maxim means. Think of it as a guiding principle: Whatever content you create should further the goal of someone knowing, liking, or trusting you more. How does someone at each stage in the "know, like, and trust" cycle interact with you and your content? And how vulnerable are you willing to be? It's important to understand that cultivating a customer relationship is similar to cultivating a personal relationship in one key way: There's a premium placed on authenticity and transparency. Introverts tend to value their privacy, and being truly transparent is a vulnerable proposition. That's why you have to decide how much of yourself you want to reveal and in what ways you want to foster the client relationship.

To help facilitate that decision process and make "know, like, and trust" content a natural part of your business, consider a moves management framework. *Moves management* is a term used in the world of nonprofit fund development. It's how fund-raising professionals describe a process by which they move an individual from being a prospective donor on the fringes of the organization to being an invested, active partner in the organization's mission.

I use this expression because I have found that attracting clients is very similar to raising money for an organization. Donors—and in our case, clients or customers—move through a process that is established by the organization. If the strategy is clear and intentional and the organization knows exactly who it wants to attract, each touch point is designed to shift the relationship to a deeper level of connection. For nonprofits, the lowest level of engagement is awareness of the organization's existence and being on the mailing list. The highest level is a donor who makes a planned gift (allotting part of the donor's estate to the organization upon the donor's death).

The donor is not necessarily aware of the process going on behind the scenes. If it's all done smoothly, the donor moves from level to level rather seamlessly and completely of her own volition. This is not about manipulating someone into doing something against her will or best interests; it's about creating an intentional pathway from initial curiosity to a mutually beneficial relationship.

The same is true for your prospective clients. A well-designed moves management process outlines clear steps for you to take (and clear content for you to create) that transitions a client from casual to convinced. Just as you don't ask someone you just met to marry you, you don't hand someone your business card, then ask him to purchase your platinum package. The introvert approach is to ease into the relationship slowly, allowing both parties to assess its potential as it develops. Working from a clear process and framework frees up your energetic resources for delivering—instead of just selling—your services and products.

The Funnel of Engagement

It may be helpful to visualize the moves management process as a funnel. The top of the funnel is wide open, reaching a large number of prospective clients with general content. As more selective people deepen their connection with you, the funnel becomes more refined and customized. There are four primary phases in the funnel of engagement: casual, connected, committed, and convinced.

Casual

- Investment: free
- Blog, articles, quotes, freebies, resources, bookstore, social media

Offerings in the Casual phase determine a prospect's first impression of you; they begin the journey of someone knowing, liking, and trusting you. They require no financial investment and very little investment of time or energy on the part of the prospect. There is potential for interaction (likes, comments, sharing), but the prospect engages without any expectation that someone will follow up with her or try to make a sale.

In general, unless the prospect makes a comment or is required to provide her email to access information, she can remain an anonymous lurker (something that, as an introvert, we can understand). People are getting to know you at this stage; they are standing on the edge of the pool, dipping their toe in the water, deciding whether or not to take the plunge.

While there is little energy investment on the part of the prospect, there is a fairly significant energy investment required of you. Carefully consider how much you want to feed the free monster. For instance, when I started doing podcasts, I published one per week. Each podcast took me between three and five hours per week to produce from start to finish. That's an incredible investment to make consistently over time (because it wasn't just the editing; it was finding interviewees, preparing questions, conducting the actual interview, and then promoting the finished product). Once I had churned out enough podcasts to have a nice library of content, I scaled back to publishing about twice per month. My learning curve also shortened, so I spent only about three hours total on each podcast. Creating content is satisfying and a great way to reach people, but make sure you do it with your energetic needs and other priorities in mind.

Connected

- Investment: minimal
- Workshops, speaking, teleclasses, radio show, podcast, newsletter, book

Products and services in this phase of the funnel require more direct communication and connection, but the content is still one-to-many. While it may seem initially labor intensive to develop these offerings, they can be more efficiently replicated and delivered than the content you offered in the Casual phase. Your offerings in the Connected phase reflect your expertise in a deeper way than at Casual, and they can be used in one of two ways: (1) Give the client enough DIY (do-it-yourself) information that she can take it from there, or (2) give the client enough information that she is inspired, curious, and made aware of the benefits of moving to the Committed phase.

At a certain point, the prospect declares herself and decides to share her information in return for this higher level of interaction from you. There is usually an exchange of value, typically of money, an email address, contact info, or more information about that person, such as the story that brought her to you (what pain point led her to seek you out). Awareness of you and your products and services is growing, and the prospect is deciding if she likes you.

Committed

- Investment: meaningful
- Hired for coaching, consulting, advising, training, service/product delivery

In the Committed phase, the interaction and content shifts from one-to-many to one-to-one. After getting to know and like you, the client has decided to trust you. The commitment is deeper and more personal. This is where some of your introvert strengths will shine: your comfort with one-on-one conversations, listening skills, and preference for diving into a topic. You're working together through coaching, consulting, advising, mentoring, or providing direct custom services/products. The information you provide is tailored and the relationship is formalized through an agreement or contract. You have structured yet flexible service/product packages that include terms, deliverables, and clear expectations.

Convinced

- Investment: significant
- High-end, premium programs and offerings, long-term relationships, referrals, advocates

Working with a client in the Convinced phase is the ultimate result of her knowing, liking, and trusting you. All of the information and content you've created has led to this point. She is convinced that you and your business are the right fit for her needs long term (which is relative to your business—it could be months or years). She becomes an advocate and a source of quality referrals. She's in love! You are delivering your highest level of services and products, in terms of quality, customization, and financial investment. At this point, it's less about you asking for the sale and more about the client asking if you'd be willing to take her on.

As you create content, consider where it fits into your funnel of engagement. Communicate clear benefits to your prospects and have a compelling call to action appropriate to where they are in the funnel. Your story and message are the backbone of everything you create. Within every level of engagement, you have an opportunity to communicate and educate your prospects on how you can solve their problems.

Each step in the process also serves as a way of calling forward your strengths and what you want to bring to other people. *And* these steps don't stop being part of your strategy once someone becomes your client. In order to maintain trust, it's important that your client continue to feel she knows and likes you. From every single external and internal perspective, your authenticity will determine your success. You don't want them looking at you a few months into your agreement and thinking the proverbial "You're not the person I married."

Where Can I Find Good Content Ideas?

Once you've made the decision to make content delivery a critical aspect of your business and a strategy has been determined, the first question is usually, "Where do I get good ideas, and get them consistently?" As an introvert, you have sharp powers of observation and a natural curiosity that lends itself well to gathering information and making it useful for your business.

Great ideas for content are all around you. You don't have to force it; it's not about being clever, funny, smart, ingenious, or off-the-charts different. The most compelling content—the kind that will get the attention of your ideal client—is authentic, useful, connected to his or her concerns, and thought-provoking.

Once you set the intention to be curious and open to information, ideas will come from all directions. You'll have so many, you'll have to start keeping a running list to make sure you capture them all. (Always, always, always carry around a small notebook—Moleskines are great!—to write down ideas as they come to you; you think you'll remember them, but you won't.) I've gotten ideas from candy wrappers, being stranded on the highway, my favorite television show, bumper stickers, jewelry, and poetry. It's when you're not looking that the best ideas come to you.

As more and more ideas come to you, begin to organize them into a logical, systematic format. This approach works especially well for blogs and social media postings. Create an editorial calendar that includes content ideas that are time-sensitive (such as New Year's or the first day of spring) as well as "evergreen" content that can be plugged in anywhere, anytime (including when you need a break or are on vacation).

Here are a few everyday resources that will help you become an idea factory. (For a complete list, see the Resources section of TheIntrovertEntrepreneur.com.)

Clients: You are witness every day to stories, breakthroughs, insights, and interactions that give an intimate view of your work. Use stories directly with permission or anonymously.

News stories/headlines: Use relevant, current events as a hook into your specific message.

Quotes: Look for inspiration among your favorite quotes, including provocative, timely, or contrary statements.

Lessons learned: Share your own lessons and/or those of others in your field or among your clients.

Response to someone else's blog, book, quote: Post a review, an opposing opinion, or offer an alternative yet agreeable perspective.

From Inspiration to Implementation

Now that you have a notebook full of ideas, how are you going to bring them to life? There is a wide range of options for sharing information that fills various points of the funnel of engagement. Even more ideas will come to you as you receive feedback from others and familiarize yourself with what the thought leaders in your field are producing. (Hint: Set up an "info@" or "news@" email account for yourself, and use that as your subscription/sign-up account for people whose promotional emails you want to receive.)

Keep in mind, you don't have to do all of these ideas. Pick a few that align with your energy, vision, resources, and strategy. Focus on quality over quantity. Give yourself space and grace to have a little research-and-development time to see what works and what doesn't. Treat your introvert energy as your most valuable currency. If you make choices that support your energetic needs, you're more likely to create a sustainable, successful plan for your business. And don't become too attached to the outcome; you may love doing teleclasses and be very good at it, but if your potential clients aren't responding to them and/or they are not meeting the definition of success you've established, teleclasses are probably not the best use of your time. Walk through open doors rather than trying to bang down closed ones.

Here are a few examples of content that you could be delivering on behalf of your message. Don't simply pull out the obvious and dismiss the more unusual choices; consider one by one how each strategy could support creatively reaching your prospects and clients. Consider also which ideas energize you and which feel like they're going to draw down your resources. (For a complete list, see the Resources section of TheIntrovertEntrepreneur.com.)

Interviews with experts. Find experts in your field or experts in your niche and interview them for a blog, vlog, radio show, podcast, or article.

Your topic 101 series. Develop a content series of very basic information for your niche. Deliver via teleclass, articles, blog, or whatever works for you. Remember that basics are good. Not everyone knows what you know, and if they know it, they usually appreciate new perspectives on old information!

Books. Writing and (self- or traditional) publishing a book is an essential element of your business if you want to be paid to speak or be presented by others for conferences, workshops, and other professional gatherings.

e-Books. An option that is inexpensive to produce and distribute and allows you to create content in smaller chunks and develop it over time.

e-Courses. Using audio, video, and/or text to lead your clients through a specific topic over a period of time (days or weeks). Could be real-time or on-demand.

Special reports, white papers, case studies. Short documents that present a problem and offer solutions to help people make decisions. They often make the case, directly or indirectly, that your services are the solution.

Home-study courses. Self-directed content for your clients that allows them to use online resources to work at their own pace.

Retreats. Facilitated experiences that are generally held over a few days at an off-site location, focused on delivering information in a highly personalized, experiential manner.

Speaking. Every day brings opportunities for public speaking. Seek out chances to speak to a local service club (Rotary, Kiwanis, etc.), local professional associations, host your own event or meet-up, or join Toastmasters. Develop three to four strong topics, create a speaker sheet, and put yourself out there! (More on this in Chapter 6.)

Internet radio. Using BlogTalkRadio or another online format, produce a show that airs at a specific time and is available for download. You have complete control over your show. These can be revenue-generating if you seek sponsorships, have advertisers, or charge guests to be part of the show.

Consider this as you develop content: As an introvert, there's a high probability that you do your best brainstorming in solitude. However, we can be left staring at a blank page, our wheels spinning because we have nothing to react to. Many of my clients have found that they are more creative if they have some structure. It frees them up from thinking about all of the components or logistics of an idea. Instead, they can follow their instincts and imagination. As part of the online resources, you'll find a worksheet I created that will be a useful tool for guiding you through the key areas of content creation. If you are less linear, consider mind mapping or drawing your ideas.

Defining Success on Your Own Terms

Physician Susan Biali, author of *Live a Life You Love*, was intensely connected to her role as a doctor. She had achieved outward success by being at the top of her class and being selected for a prestigious residency. However, her internal definition of success wasn't aligned with her external accomplishments. She realized she wasn't excited about her daily life; it was something to be "gotten through." That led her to clarify what success meant to her: "Today, success is having significant aspects of my life that make me really excited about my life as it is right now, but then always moving towards some wonderful experiences that I hope to create for myself in the future."

An underlying message throughout this book is that you can create success on your own terms, in a way that honors and respects your introvert personality. When it comes to anything in entrepreneurship—planning, marketing, networking, systems, collaborations, product development—one-size-fits-all advice can lead you down a rocky road.

This is especially true when it comes to your marketing activities. If there's anything that I've seen introverts express frustration about, it's the slick, almost over-the-top approach that they see so many others doing . . . and they wonder, "Should I be doing that, too, even if it feels gross?" After all, it must work or else others wouldn't be doing it!

Perhaps those techniques work for them, but that doesn't mean they'll work for you. If you don't feel authentic in the messages you're putting out, your prospect will pick up on that.

Success is one of those words that is thrown around by entrepreneurs without much thought as to what it actually means. Of course, we all want success. We can probably all agree that if you look at success as the opposite of failure, there's an element of universal understanding around the word. But that's about as far as it goes. Defining success is as complex and individual as you are.

In fact, you may be carrying around a definition of success that you inherited from your parents, teachers, friends, mentors, bosses, or colleagues. That borrowed definition might center around money, title, power, memberships, awards, publications, or even how many people wave at you when you walk down the street.

These are all societal markers of success—and there's nothing inherently wrong with any of them. It's OK to say we want to make a certain amount of money or belong within a particular circle of people. However, introverts may be equally driven by internal or less tangible rewards. We appreciate external and tangible validation, but we know that it simply represents an outward manifestation of the success we feel on the inside.

As Dan Pink writes in *Drive: The Surprising Truth About What Motivates Us*, people aren't as motivated by the reward-and-punishment approach as previously thought. Rather, they find reward in having three things in place: autonomy, mastery, and purpose.

Autonomy: The freedom to march to the beat of your own drummer. You are independent, not beholden to someone else's vision.

Mastery: Becoming the best in the world at what you do.

Purpose: Making a difference to other people, their processes, or the planet.

Consider each of those in turn. Chances are you chose an entrepreneurial path because you were seeking at least one, if not all, of these three traits. As an introvert, you most likely place a high value on working at your own pace, drawing on your inner world for creativity and insight. Introverts also like to immerse themselves in topics or tasks rather than spreading themselves too thin. And while most everyone craves a sense of purpose in their work, it's even more important that the introvert recognize the role purpose plays in his business. After all, you are expending energy to make it work, and if you're continually asking yourself, "What's the point?" you'll wear yourself out because the motivation is based more in material—rather than meaningful—rewards.

You won't be successful in your marketing efforts until you find out what motivates you. For me, success is defined as freedom. It's freedom *from* (worry, stress, boredom, compromise) and freedom *to* (do, say, act, give, create, receive). I've learned that I am highly motivated by autonomy, followed closely by mastery of my craft and living with a sense of purpose and mission.

How do you define success? Is it a feeling? A freedom? A tangible result? A certain confidence or knowing? Once you know your overall definition of success, you can set intentional goals not only for your marketing efforts but everything else in your life.

What's It Worth to You?

> *You can only become truly accomplished at something you love. Don't make money your goal. Instead, pursue the things you love doing, and then do them so well that people can't take their eyes off you.* —Maya Angelou

We choose an entrepreneurial path so that we can follow our passion. We want to share our natural gifts, learn new skills, and stretch ourselves for the benefit of our clients. It's so much fun, and sometimes so easy, we could do it even if we never made a dime.

Yay for us if we're doing work we love! But here's the thing: You own a business, not a hobby. Your business is what you pursue professionally. One of your objectives is to reap a financial return for the work you do (remember, one of the defining characteristics of entrepreneurship is to make a profit). You can love that work to the point where you can't believe that you get paid to do it. That's the great benefit of entrepreneurship. You get paid to do what you love to do. If you didn't, it would be an avocation: something outside your profession, done purely for the love of it.

Because of the L-word—*love*—the lines between vocation and

avocation can become very blurry. This is especially true if you have any level of fear or doubt about the value of your products or services or talking about the value of your services with others. If not addressed, that fear can quickly turn a business into a hobby.

There are several criteria one could use for deciding if what you're doing is a business or a hobby, but for our purposes, I'm going to stick with the financial aspect of things. Most specifically, are you charging—and charging adequately—for the content and services you're offering?

When you're first starting out, it's natural to value experience over money. You want to get a few clients on your roster, some positive testimonials, and make your "mistakes" (that is, learn from your experiences) before the stakes are too high. In my case, I was offering a certain amount of pro bono coaching to accumulate both experience and hours for my certification.

It's also valuable to offer a few sample products or services for free. I gave teleclasses, webinars, and workshops for free during the first two years of my business. They offered tremendous opportunity to start developing content and be in an R&D (research and development) phase. I received feedback that helped me to refine my offerings, along with testimonials and confidence. It's one thing to be on the safe "before" side of the experience and say "I'm going to offer a workshop"; it's another thing to stand on the other side of having offered it and be able to say with confidence "I did it!"

In the beginning, free offerings are expected and can serve as a valuable learning lab for you and your business. Confidence matters more than cash, and kudos keep your spirits up.

There comes a turning point, however, when you acknowledge that you're ready for more than kudos and the warm, fuzzy feelings they inspire. Sure, you can take one more class, give one more trial-run workshop, write two more articles, accumulate ten more hours . . . and for successful entrepreneurs, the learning never ends. But it can become an excuse that keeps you from taking action.

Making the transition from hobby mode to business mode is essential. You must learn to value what you have to offer enough that you don't give it away.

I learned a fabulous reframe of the role of money in business from introvert entrepreneur Tshombe Brown. During a workshop I attended, he shared his personal philosophy, which will stay with me forever: Having created something that's worth your investment of time, it becomes a win-win when I give you the opportunity to express your appreciation for what I have offered through financial means. In other words, if I give away my products and information, I'm denying you the opportunity to share your gratitude for what you've received.

Charging for your offerings and services is an acknowledgment that it's worth the person's investment of time and money and that you worked hard to create that worth.

As the saying goes, we teach others how we want to be treated. This might not be the most obvious perspective for the introvert; it requires that we develop an awareness of what we're projecting to others, which means taking an external look at ourselves (rather than the internal one that we're used to). We have to notice what signals we're putting out about how other people should respond to us.

Consider the following when faced with the question of placing a value on your products or services:

Ask for what you want. If you soft-peddle your invitation and your desire to attract people to your business, you give them an out, which they'll take! If you want people to show up or to buy from you, it's important to give them a clear and confident invitation as well as a solid reason (the benefit and added value to them) to show up.

Trust the value of your individual voice. Your offer is valuable because no one else can say it exactly like you. You put tremendous pressure on yourself if you make the assumption that an offering has to be groundbreaking to be valuable. In reality, it's not a radical, never-heard-before thought that will differentiate you from the pack; it's your confidence in your message and your ability to share it with the right people at the right time.

You always have choices. When you feel like you have no choices, you're allowing fear-based thinking to have the power. This is an opportunity to begin a new practice of honoring your value by determining your prices not based on what others are doing but based on your intention and your belief in the value of the offering.

You can handle whatever happens. The answer to any fearful "if statement" you can conjure up is, "I can handle it." If you are too attached to a particular outcome, you'll consider anything less than as a failure. A healthier approach is to be curious: "I wonder what's going to happen." You choose to trust that whatever happens, you can handle it. You'll learn and grow from it.

Ask for what you want. (Yes, you read that right—again. We can never hear this one too many times.) When we come from a place of confidence and ask for what we want, we help people feel invited and needed. They appreciate the mutual exchange of value. We all come away from the transaction feeling like we received what we needed.

Finding the Middle Ground

There's one more angle from which you can choose to view the sales process: cultivating your ambivert energy. Ambiverts are people who fall in the middle of the introvert–extrovert spectrum. They feel an equal comfort with and desire for socializing and solitude. Recent research, conducted by Adam Grant of the Wharton School of the University of Pennsylvania, supports a balanced approach, one that demonstrates the value of drawing on both your introvert and extrovert energies.

Grant administered a personality survey to more than three hundred people, and then tracked their sales records for three months. He began with the hypothesis that extroverts, rather than outperforming their more introverted counterparts, would report less-than-stellar results. He was proven right. People who fell on the extremes of the introvert–extrovert spectrum were outproduced by those who fell more in the middle. Ambiverts earned 24 percent more in sales than did introverts, and 32 percent more than extroverts. According to Grant, "Because they naturally engage in a flexible pattern of talking and listening, ambiverts are likely to express sufficient assertiveness and enthusiasm to persuade and close a sale but are more inclined to listen to customers' interests and less vulnerable to appearing too excited or overconfident."[2]

How is this information useful to introvert entrepreneurs? First, it shows that introverts already have a head start when it comes to sales; your typical buyer is more likely to be turned off by someone who talks too much than by someone who listens too much. Second, most of us are at least flirting with ambivert tendencies rather than being on the extremes. That means you probably just have to sharpen a latent extroverted skill you already have, rather than starting from zero. And finally, it helps us to release the expectation that one must be incredibly outgoing and have the gift of gab to be an effective salesperson. It's an invitation to listen twice as much as we talk, which comes naturally to most introverts (after all, as the Greek philosopher Epictetus reminded us, "We have two ears and one mouth so that we can listen twice as much as we speak").

Introvert Entrepreneur Focus

John E. Doerr, co-president of RAIN Group and bestselling author of *Insight Selling: Surprising Research on What Sales Winners Do Differently*

You've studied what separates the people who make the sale from those who don't. What has your research shown?

The biggest thing we saw sales winners do differently than second-place finishers was provide new insights and ideas. It used to be that I relied on the seller to tell me about their products and services, because I couldn't find all of that information on my own. But buyers are more sophisticated today; they have access to so much more information now because of the Internet.

The seller has become part of the value equation. They're part of the value that somebody is buying, and that's part of what differentiates them.

The second biggest thing that we saw is that sales winners collaborated in the sales process. So they're not doing it *to* the buyer, they're doing something *with* the buyer to come up with a solution that will make the buyer's world better, however they think of it, whether it's business, personal, or a combination of both.

Introverts are definitely drawn to entrepreneurship, but they're not always enamored of that sales process. They want to focus on providing their service and product rather than on selling it. What have you learned about successful sales that can be useful to the sales-adverse introvert?

They have to get away from the perception of the perfect seller as the person who is out there shaking hands and the idea of the always happy, jovial, can-make-friends-with-anybody kind of seller. Introverts also tend to be insightful by nature, they tend to be very introspective, they listen well, they can analyze what they hear, and come out with the solution.

Selling isn't just about being pushy and forcing people to buy. If introverts play to that strength of connecting the dots for somebody and providing the solution based on their knowledge and their insights, that can really help them.

How can an introvert leverage those strengths to feel more confident at sales and develop an approach that feels congruent?

As an entrepreneur, maybe you invented something, maybe you started something new. Your ability to put things down on paper and teach and present is one way of attracting buyers to you.

Rather than having to push all the time, you can do a pull strategy: start writing, start talking, start presenting. As we know, some of the best actors and public speakers are actually introverts.

They use the stage as a way to get across what is important to them. They have an inner ambition that says, "I will make the leap for this moment to go out and meet new people and talk, because I believe in my product, I believe in my company, I believe in what I have to offer." At the same time, be careful not to use your label as an introvert as an excuse not to do other important sales activities, such as networking, because we both know that it's possible to go beyond the traditional mold of how an introvert reaches out to the world.

Chapter 6

It Takes a Village

Whether you call them your tribe, platform, network, community, or peeps, you need people to create a strong and sustainable business. Yes, even introvert entrepreneurs need people around them in order to succeed! As the leader of a particular community of clients, customers, and colleagues, we can't operate in a vacuum, and we can't isolate more than we engage. There's certainly room for us to close the door, turn off the phone, and give ourselves a break from the hustle and bustle. But more than ever before, entrepreneurs are expected to be highly engaged with their clients and customers. The rise of social media dictates that we be consistent, transparent, and available.

But for introverts, there is a flip side to this: The more people we have involved in our lives, the more potential there is for our energy to be sucked into the black hole of no return. Notice that I said "potential." It's not a certainty. Just as we can feel a spark from interacting with our spouses, partners, or best friends, we can be energized by having the right people around us.

That's where your peeps come in. The trick is finding out who they are, the best way to reach them, and how to engage with them once you've found them.

Your tribe isn't necessarily the same as your business colleagues and partners, although there may be some overlap. Rather, these are people you are leading. Marketing authority Seth Godin defines a tribe as a group that is connected to one another, a leader (in this case, you), and an idea (your message, mission, vision). They are people who have chosen to embrace and evangelize about you and your business. They believe in you and find value in what you're offering. They will interact with you in a thousand different ways, some of which will support your bottom line and others that will support your spirit.

On a baseline level, having a clearly defined tribe tells others who have yet to hear about you that you have a message worth hearing. You aren't just up on your soapbox talking to anyone who will listen. You are targeting your message, and it's landing on the ears of the people who need to hear it the most.

Your tribe plays an important, almost starring, role in your business. They give you feedback. They tell others about you. They allow you to be in many places at once. They show others—potential publishers, booking agents, distribution managers, product developers, investors—that you've got something that people want.

For the introvert entrepreneur, it's not just about numbers. If all we're after is more likes, friends, connections, or people in our circles, we're not making any meaningful connection to the people we've attracted. We're better off focusing on cultivating quality relationships rather than thinking it's a numbers game. I've found time and time again that if I connect with the one right person, that opens the doors to far more than I would have found if I'd focused on how many people were on my email subscriber list. Sustainable business development and tribe formation works when we understand that quantity follows quality.

The benefits of having an intentional tribe of committed, engaged fans are numerous:

Being an influencer and positioning yourself as an expert. If you want to be the go-to person on your topic, it's imperative that people know who you are and what you have to offer. That seems basic, but it's surprising how easy it is to sit back and assume people will know what you're doing if you just post a tweet once a week. Once you've found your tribe, you can focus your message and talk only to them. You want your focus to be narrow—a spotlight rather than a floodlight—so that when they hear a certain word, phrase, or problem, you are top of mind. In my case, when someone hears the word *introvert*, I want them to think of me. The more that happens, the more I know my message is reaching the right ears.

Efficient one-to-many communication. While engaging with people one-on-one is a strength for most introverts, it can also be a labor-intensive way to share your message. In the beginning, you will probably have more coffee dates than speaking engagements. But as your business grows and your message is refined, you'll want to find ways to reach more people as efficiently as possible. Your tribe becomes your built-in audience, ready and eager for your information.

Receiving feedback and being responsive. This is especially true of the virtual tribe that you'll build through social media channels. They become an informal focus group for all of the messages that you put out there. They're a fairly safe group with whom you can play a bit of "mad scientist," testing out different approaches to see what comes to life. Based on their response (or lack thereof), you're getting invaluable feedback about your products, services, brand, and presence in the marketplace. In return, you have the opportunity to engage in conversation and further establish yourself as the go-to person in your field. You can be responsive to what's being shared without a huge expenditure of energy or time. For instance, if someone asks you a question on your Facebook timeline, chances are high that others have the same question. You can answer that post personally and in the moment, meeting the needs of not just the poster but anyone else who's "listening" in to the conversation.

Space to build "know, like, and trust." As we explored in Chapter 5, people do business with people they know, like, and trust. Simply by the process of intentionally creating a tribe, you are inviting people into your inner realm. This is not always easy for introvert entrepreneurs. What we have to understand is that our work is making our internal world external. It's an outward expression of our inner being, a safe and even tender place we dwell that doesn't get exposed that often. That makes it vulnerable. I've found that few things inspire more response and more connection than allowing myself to be vulnerable with people. It's not about being overly sensitive or emotional; it's about being real with people. You simply tell the truth. You place a high value on transparency and communication. You show that you're human. It takes practice and involves a bit of risk, but the payoff is worth it.

There are multiple ways to build a tribe, and we're going to focus on the tools and techniques that make the most of the natural strengths and energy needs of the introvert entrepreneur:

- Social media networks and virtual offerings
- Blogging and writing
- Public speaking and presentations

Social Media Networks and Virtual Offerings

It used to be, as recently as seven years ago, that if your business didn't have a website, it didn't exist. Now, if you don't have a presence on Facebook, Twitter, Google+, LinkedIn, etc., you don't exist. The number of virtual tribe-building platforms seems to increase by the day, and it's easy to get sucked into all of them without an intention or strategy in place.

It's totally without irony that I refer to social media sites as "bright shiny objects." They glisten with promise, they flash "Join us!" at every turn, and they promise connection and community. Who wouldn't be seduced by that! But in truth, even though you're not face to face, they are another form of interaction that requires your energy. It's what makes social media (and by extension, the web) the greatest thing to happen to introverts since Carl Jung: We get to pace ourselves and engage in a more deliberate way. As Jennifer B. Kahnweiler, author of *The Genius of Opposites*, shared with me, "In my experience, introverts really use social media with conscious intent. They're thoughtful." She goes on to say that in her interviews with introverted leaders, she found that they tended to choose a platform that resonated most with them, then really learned to use it.

The flip side of this desire to focus is that as the number of social media outlets increase, there are more and more bright shiny objects competing for your time and attention, and that can lead to all of those good intentions going right out the window.

In a moment I'll share some thoughts on the most dominant social media platforms today. By the time you have this book in your hands (or on your screen), the landscape will have shifted in ways large and small. Because of that, we won't go far down the "which tool should I use, and how should I use it?" road. Technology changes too quickly, and there are other important points to cover about social media—and our use of technology in general— that are platform independent. Let's start there.

Why You Don't Have to—and Shouldn't— Chase Down Every Bright Shiny Object

> Technology . . . the knack of so arranging the world that
> we don't have to experience it.   —Max Frisch

A few years ago, I attended an event called BizTechDay Seattle. The room was full of geeky people, like me, who love new technology and gadgets and programs that are supposed to make our lives more efficient, fun, or connected. In between speakers, there were demonstrations of technologies we didn't know existed but, now that we knew of their existence, we *had* to have.

I left that day overwhelmed by all of the bright shiny objects I'd learned about and wondered (OK, salivated) about how I was going to implement what I'd learned.

Fortunately, I didn't do any of it.

As I've done before, I'm going to reference Jim Collins's classic *Good to Great* through the lens of the introvert entrepreneur. You might think that a chapter about technology in a book published in 2001 wouldn't have much insight or relevance in our Facebook/Twitter/LinkedIn/iPhone world.

And you would be wrong. If anything, it's even more relevant.

During the course of their research, Collins and his team found that the use of technology was a key factor that differentiated the great companies from the good.

What Was the Difference?

Collins found that the great companies used technology as an accelerator, not a creator, of momentum. They used it to take a concept or product that already existed and make it better. They didn't adopt new technology gratuitously or to create something new; they used it to leverage their core mission. They only employed technology purposefully and strategically, not falling under the spell of bright shiny objects.

The good to great companies took a "crawl, walk, run" approach to technology. Their choices were based on sustainability and the degree to which each type of technology aligned with their core competencies and products. The comparison companies went in reverse, running before they could walk or even crawl. They reacted to what others were doing, for fear of being left behind.

See how this works?

So often, I hear, "If I just had the right program, software, smartphone, or computer, things would be so much better."

Or "That's so cool . . ." (looking at a new social media platform that does everything but go to the doctor for you). "I'm going to make my profile and the clients will come knocking!"

Or "You *have* to be on Twitter, Facebook, LinkedIn, or else you'll have no credibility."

There's something many people are realizing, now that the shine has dulled slightly on these miracle tools (and for introverts, they are definitely miraculous). We're learning what this type of technology for introvert entrepreneurs is . . . and is not.

It is not our knight in shining armor. We can't depend on technology to save the day, or to protect us from doing stuff we often avoid (such as picking up the phone). It might bring us some efficiencies, it might pave the way to more comfortable interactions, but it's not a magic bullet.

It is not a substitute for human contact. Sure, we can form relationships online, but the magic happens when we meet eye to eye. Technology should not *define* our relationships; rather, it should enhance what exists in the real world. We can use it strategically as a bridge between someone being a faceless, personality-less name on a piece of paper to being a human being standing in front of us.

It is a seductive mistress. We can wrap ourselves around a new toy and find a way to fit it into our business, because, hey, it's super cool and we want to be cutting edge! If it's not in service to our primary mission, if it's not obvious how it's going to make our work more efficient or effective, if it's just going to be a cool distraction that keeps us feeling busy, then the tail's wagging the dog. Technology should enhance and advance our goals, not determine them.

It is a drain on your resources. When we hear we *have* to do something or else be regarded as a social media pariah, we end up posting profiles and creating new accounts on platforms that we don't possibly have time to sustain. We plant a million seeds and expect them to grow without any water.

What's more important than jumping on the latest gadget craze is to pick a few strategic tools that make the most of your time, energy, and money. Be sure they are in alignment with your company's values and business priorities, and then show up 100 percent.

We all love bright shiny objects—they're part of what makes life happy and fun. We have unprecedented and largely equal access to a million different tools. Choose yours based on what brings you closer to your definition of excellence, what's sustainable, and what works in service to you, your energy, and your goals.

The 35,000-Foot View of the Social Media Landscape

The web isn't magic, it's merely efficient.

—Seth Godin

The specific tools that people are using online to connect, promote, and conduct business are a moving target. There are some that seem to be here for the duration: Facebook, Twitter, and LinkedIn are the Triumphant Trio of Social Media. They have adapted themselves to changing trends and are, in fact, shaping the trends themselves.

Each platform's community has a different culture and reason for being. For instance, Facebook and Twitter are hybrid personal–

professional sites. You can use them for either purpose, and both tolerate a mixture of sharing what you ate for breakfast and how people can sign up for your next workshop. LinkedIn is much more professionally oriented. Profiles and discussions are focused on business topics, only occasionally touching on the personal. Unlike other more casual platforms, if you decided to share in your LinkedIn status update that you mowed your lawn this weekend, you would be revealing a lack of understanding of the platform's central purpose.

Here are some questions to take into account as you strategize which social media platforms are going to give you the highest return on investment (of time, money, energy):

Where does your tribe hang out? There are multiple factors to take into account: age, profession, ethnicity, geographic location, politics, religion, marital status, hobbies. Some social networking sites cater to specific interests and demographics, while others (such as Facebook) cast a wide net and allow people to put themselves into niche groups. Check to see how easy it is to interact with people on the site as well as how targeted you can be with your interactions. For instance, Facebook Pages and Groups are highly specific, and using Twitter hashtags can help focus your message to certain people looking for information on a particular topic, even if the tweet stream is busy.

How available do you want to be? To be most effective, rapid-fire platforms like Twitter require faster response times and more consistent engagement than the relatively slower-paced Facebook. LinkedIn allows for even more breathing room.

How credible is the platform? Not all social networking sites are created equal. Does it have a history of stability, flexibility, and responsiveness to its users? Do other entrepreneurs have a presence there, especially your peers and competitors? What is the quality of the postings and conversation?

How easy is the platform to use, both from your and the user's perspective? If you have challenges setting up a profile or figuring out what you're supposed to do once you've signed up, chances are your prospects and peeps will be challenged, too. The platform should be intuitive, friendly, and as free from spam as possible (while spam is impossible to avoid altogether, there should be evidence that the site managers don't tolerate it). Ideally, the site should be free for at least a basic profile and services.

How popular is the platform, and does it facilitate easy sharing of content? A beautiful, intuitive social media site is useless unless it's well integrated with the rest of the web through plug-ins, add-ons, toolbar shortcuts, and sharing buttons on major sites. This is the way content goes viral, and it makes it easy for others to spread the word about your business. For the introvert, this is a huge advantage because it facilitates a wider reach with less effort than was required before the dot-com explosion.

Is the focus of the platform on business, personal, or both? Depending on the image and purpose of your business, you will either draw a bright line between personal and professional, or the line will be blurred. For instance, as a coach, I blur the line. I am my business (at least until I hire my first employee), and whether or not people like me is a big part of how they'll decide if I'm a good fit for them. So while my strategy includes promoting my business, I also allow my personality to come through.

Life in the Fishbowl

Living in a fishbowl—with your every move on display for the world—is no longer reserved for movie stars and faux reality TV celebrities. Social media has taken information that used to be private or shared among a close circle of friends and provided space for it to be broadcast to the world.

You have to decide how much of yourself to share as part of your social media strategy. Introverts tend to be more private and reserved, given our more internal orientation. There's definite risk with being vulnerable online, because we're making the internal external, and it lives there forever. I've also heard a lot of introverts say, "I'm an introvert in real life, but an extrovert online. I can be social, as long as I'm at home in my jammies with my laptop, cat, and cup of tea." They don't feel vulnerable as much as they feel liberated. After all, just because social interaction can wear us out doesn't mean we don't have a strong need for connection and community.

Nor should this cause us to feel like we have a split personality. The truth is, we are a mix of introvert and extrovert. We have both energies within us. Much of how we show up energetically has to do with how safe we feel in our environment. If we've chosen our online networks wisely, and used discretion about the people we allow to have access, we will feel a fairly high degree of safety. We can share more of ourselves and allow the divide between personal and professional to be a bit more porous. Social media can be less draining because the socializing we do is less immediate, more controlled.

My rule of thumb: If my personal beliefs, preferences, or activities influence why or how I deliver my services, they're worth sharing. It's probably wise to refrain from sharing opinions on controversial topics, but if it's integral to who you are (such as sharing your faith or political beliefs) and you're OK with it becoming information people can use to self-select (either in or out), that is your choice. Do you bring your religion, politics, work history, parental or marital status, sexual orientation, education, or personal hobbies into your work? Do you draw on those experiences in working with customers or clients? Is sharing those experiences in service to your tribe and their needs—or is it merely satisfying your ego? It's always a good idea to be clear with yourself about your motivations for sharing. Just because you can share doesn't mean you should. But if it connects you to your audience and helps them self-select, it might be worth the risk.

Bridging from Online to IRL Relationships

At some point, you're going to do a live event or bring people together in person for a great new offering or product . . . and you'll discover that everyone you've been hanging out with is virtual. You know their avatars, but you don't know *them*.

The relative comfort and ease of making connections online can turn into stress when you realize that those connections are fleeting, dependent on the whims of a platform developer or the latest trends in social media. For example, consider when Facebook started out. It wasn't too crowded, your wall was simple, ads were few, and people were more discriminating about who they accepted as friends. It was more about friendly connection and sharing photos and updates.

Now the user interface has evolved many times over, making it much more challenging to be seen and heard amid the chatter. Posts may or may not be seen, depending on the user's settings. People who decided to treat Facebook as their website found they were at the mercy of the company's policies, updates, and formatting changes. It's almost impossible to build a consistent, reliable brand presence when your platform is a moving target.

That's why it's important to be cultivating your flesh-and-blood tribe alongside your virtual tribe. You do not want to rely on a social media platform for the bulk of your engagement, or as your primary web presence. It's easy to allow that to happen; as we've outlined, communicating online has its definite advantages for the introvert. It's also easier to jump on board a moving train in which most of the structure and community is ready-made for you. You might be tempted to hitch your wagon to their star; don't. Not only will you be giving them too much control over your brand, you will end up investing a disproportionate amount of time and energy in maintaining your online connections, to the possible detriment of your off-line tribe.

That said, we can still leverage technology as a link between our virtual tribe and real-life connections. Go back to the content ideas we explored in Chapter 5. Which ones would translate well into a podcast, video, webinar, or teleclass? Building your platform through these methods enables you to control the communication environment, scripting out or targeting your content while building in as little or as much interaction as you want.

This is a good first step toward making a personal connection with the people you hang out with online. It puts you in the driver's seat while offering increased value to your connections. Choose the medium that you feel most comfortable with. For instance, I enjoy podcasting because I get to interview interesting people (one at a time!); talk about topics that I feel passionately about; prepare for the conversation in advance; then record, edit, and post it according to my own standards and timetable. There's a focused burst of energy required to make the podcast happen, but once I publish and share it, it can more or less walk on its own. I don't need to hold its hand (unless I choose to keep promoting it alongside other pieces of content).

The value of the podcast and other similar media is that they enable you to step closer to your prospects through your voice and image, not just your words. The potential for them to know, like, and trust you is dramatically increased if they literally see and hear you in action. Conversely, they can more quickly discern if your message isn't a good fit for them, thereby self-selecting out of your prospect pool.

Once you've increased your interaction with people, you can start to discern those with whom you'd like to cultivate a more personal relationship. Take a look at your contacts through Facebook, LinkedIn, Twitter, Google+, even Pinterest, to see who appears to have business goals similar or complementary to your own. The typical profiles will reveal how long they've been in business, their previous professional history, and their connections. Depending on how thoroughly they've completed a profile, you can gain information about their reading habits, hobbies, and social activities. Remember to cross-reference the profiles to get the complete picture.

If someone seems to be in sync with you, your business, and values, reach out to her through the most appropriate social media platform. Suggest a coffee date if you live in the same area; if not, have "virtual coffee" over Skype or other videoconferencing service. You don't need to go into the conversation with a strict agenda. Let the other person know when you send your introductory message that you're interested in learning more about her business, in the event you can share her as a resource or otherwise support her goals. You can also say that you think your business would be a good resource for her, and you'd appreciate the opportunity to chat. There's no sales pitch involved. It's simply a get-to-know-you conversation that allows both people to determine if further conversation would be beneficial.

Online profiles and communities have been a gift to introvert entrepreneurs everywhere because they allow us to connect on our own terms. Before we go to an event, we can often see who else is going and do a little research. This can dramatically increase our comfort level with walking into a roomful of strangers. There are several ways you can find out who else will be attending. If you RSVP online, sometimes the event website includes an updated list of attendees. Events posted on LinkedIn and Facebook will also give you an idea of who will be there, even without registering. You can also share that you're attending a particular event on social media and ask who else is going. I've tried this a few times and appreciate that it serves double duty: Not only do I find out if any of my colleagues have registered, but I've shared a resource with them that they may not have known about.

Once you have a few names, look up their profiles on social media. Go into the event with a list of people you'd like to meet. This gives you a focus and a mission. It also gives you an opening line after you introduce yourself: "I was intrigued by your LinkedIn profile and your work with so-and-so. Would you have a few minutes to tell me more about it?"

Blogging and Writing:
The Introvert's Playground

There's a poster that has been widely shared on social media that says, "I write better than I talk." Introverts tend to relate to this sentiment! That's not surprising; because we process our thoughts internally and quietly, it's natural that we'd prefer the slower pace of the written word over talking through things aloud. This doesn't necessarily mean we're naturally good writers. Like any other skill, it comes easily to some and is elusive to others. The point isn't to judge yourself too harshly, but to recognize that your preference for communicating through writing can be a strong entrepreneurial asset in our content-driven world.

Blogging is one of the easiest, most accessible ways to start establishing yourself as a thought leader in your field. A blog is like an online diary or journal, and it consists of regularly posted entries that are written by you and then shared through a feed, reader, or other electronic distribution method. Your topic focus, how often you blog, and how long your posts are depend on your purpose for blogging.

Being clear about why you're blogging in the first place will enable you to connect more easily to the right people. Do you want to share tips, resources, and information? Establish your expertise and credibility through opinion pieces? Tell stories about people who use your products or services? Influence the way people perceive you, your business, or your message?

There are upward of two hundred million blogs pinging through cyberspace, which demonstrates that as a platform builder, the blog is here to stay. People appreciate its immediacy, informality, and short learning curve. Many businesses (my own included) use a blog platform as their company website. For instance, WordPress is popular, free software that enables you to go live with your blog in minutes. If you want to build a website outside of a blogging platform, it's important to integrate blogging capabilities within that site.

Blogs by nature tend to be more conversational and shorter than other forms of content sharing (such as white papers, articles, and e-books). The beauty of blogging is that you are completely in control and can determine how much you want to say, when you say it, and how you say it. A blog post can be anywhere from three hundred to twelve hundred words. Post length, along with the tone you adopt, should be guided by two things: your personal style and preference and what others in your field are doing. Look to see how your peers are using their blog. Do they take a personal tone? Are they more about statistics and facts? Do they use a lot of images, video, or both? These are good questions to ask, but they shouldn't necessarily dictate how *you* decide to create *your* blog. In fact, surveying other blogs will reveal as many practices to avoid as to adopt. While your peers' blogs provide you with a good point of reference, it's ultimately your choice as to how you approach your blog.

A few important tips for beginning and maintaining your business blog:

Be consistent. This applies to quality, perspective, timing, and topic. With so many priorities calling for your attention, it's important to find a system that works for you and your rhythm. Write as often as you can do it well, and stay on point. If possible, create a schedule for yourself that fits blogging and writing in with your other business development activities. Decide what topic areas fit your niche best and stick to them. Just because you don't have a topic one week, don't decide to write about your dog. Better to skip that post than to go off on a tangent and potentially confuse and lose your readers.

Encourage conversation. When I first started regularly communicating with my prospects, I did it through a weekly e-newsletter. It took me hours to complete the content. In return, I received feedback and comments from people individually, never publicly. That sounds like what an introvert would be most comfortable with, right? In reality, it might be comfortable, but it's not going to build your tribe. There's too much happening behind the scenes and not enough witnesses.

When I realized this, I turned to blogging instead. It was a more public way to engage people in conversation and make it easy for them to share my content through social media buttons and links. The catch is that blogging definitely opens you up to criticism and people who disagree with you. That's one of the most vulnerable parts of this process: You're sharing your knowledge and passion, and some people might not like it. There are those who know how to disagree respectfully, and then there are "trolls": those who feel good about themselves only when they are putting others down. Realize that you will get both types of comments. See it as an opportunity to gather valuable information that is outside of your usual perspective. You can use their comments to inform what roadblocks people might toss in your way. Take what is valuable, and leave the rest—especially the trolls!

Tell stories, don't pitch. Blogging is not for blatant self-promotion or to tell everyone about your latest product or special offer. The expectation from readers is that there will be information and stories, not a sales pitch. You can use your blog to share success stories of clients and customers. Give the inside scoop on how a new product is going to benefit others (while including some valuable content that gives them a taste of that benefit). Offer people tips on how to better use your services or products. Tell your own story and give others insights into who you are; it's all part of the "know, like, and trust" objective. Consider the blog an opportunity to *show, not tell.*

Release perfectionism. Blogs are informal and conversational. You want to be professional, use proper grammar, and have a well-structured post. But beware the little voice that says it has to be unique, creative, or perfect. Blogger Judy Dunn offers this advice: "Get rid of the word 'creative.' When I sit down to write, I don't want somebody standing over and telling me I better be creative, or nobody will want to read what I write. You're not coming up with a creative blog post, you're sitting down to write an interesting post that's going to be helpful to your readers."

If you're convinced a blog will benefit your outreach efforts, but you're not a natural writer, or if it feels challenging to come up with regular posts that are on topic, then consider hiring a blogging coach or consultant. These experts will guide you through the ins and outs of blogging and teach you how to use it to best position your business. However, resist the temptation to have that person ghostwrite the blog for you. The personal nature of a blog (even when it's about business) creates an expectation that your voice is the one that people are reading. If they read your blog and then meet you in person, and you come across as two different people, that's a deal breaker.

There are other options to strictly narrative blog posts, such as podcasts, image-based posts, inviting guest bloggers, or having multiple contributors to a single post (also called "reverse blogging"). Find the approach that's most comfortable and authentic for you. Not only will it help attract your ideal clients to you, but it will be easier to maintain your energy and interest in the content.

Public Speaking/Presenting

There are only two types of speakers in the world. (1) The nervous and (2) Liars. —Mark Twain

Why *Public Speaking* and *Introvert* Are Not Incompatible

Standing up in front of people, all eyes on you, everyone waiting for you to say something smart, clever, or profound—would you consider this an introvert's worst nightmare or a huge opportunity?

Just as *introvert* and *entrepreneur* might seem contradictory terms, so might *introvert* and *public speaker*. But remember the definition of introvert: It's about how we gain and drain energy. It's also about our point of reference (internal) and how we prefer to communicate, not how *well* we communicate. In reality, your introvert strengths lend themselves well to being a strong public speaker.

In fact, the specific strengths that tend to come with the introvert "package" may actually give us a valuable edge over our extrovert colleagues—if properly leveraged. For instance, our ability to read the energy of a room means we can be responsive to what people need in the moment. It may sound like a contradiction, but our penchant for thorough preparation, ironically, means that when things don't go as planned, we can adapt more quickly because our confidence level is higher. And as I've mentioned in other areas, the ability to be both prepared and flexible relies on your willingness to be unattached to specific results.

A few years ago, I facilitated a two-day workshop with a group of six dynamic, creative women, designed to help them uncover their core business vision. The curriculum was clearly outlined and shared. Participants came in knowing what would be presented and what kind of outcomes they could expect. I was prepared to follow my agenda and lead them to the promised result: a clear entrepreneurial vision statement, which would serve as a foundation for marketing and other action plans.

Within an hour of being together in that sunny, welcoming workshop space, I knew things were going to go very differently. Each person came to the weekend with a unique need and expectation. It was clear that while my agenda wouldn't be completely irrelevant, I had to release the need to stick closely to it. Instead of focusing on the *how*, I needed to focus on the *what*. My overall intention was to create a space for them to discern what was most important to them as entrepreneurs. It was that intention that needed to take precedence over a strict predetermined agenda.

But I will readily admit: As an introvert who likes to be prepared, especially when I'm presenting in front of people who expect me to know a bit more about something than they do, I was temporarily thrown for a loop. My brain scrambled to reconcile what I had on the page in front of me and what I was hearing from the participants. Then I realized it was like a dance. I had learned certain moves, and they had certain moves, and to work well together, there had to be give-and-take. I was prepared enough, with a definite emphasis on "enough." I knew my material and my intention, and I was confident in the value of my offering. That enabled me to release my attachment to whatever was on the page and listen to my colleagues. We ended up co-creating a powerful experience for one another. Each person came away with valuable insights, and I came away knowing I could be flexible because I had gone in confidently prepared and open to the group.

Another introvert strength—or perhaps it's more accurate to call it an advantage—is that we catch people by surprise. They don't expect an introvert to be a powerful speaker. As Jim Collins has written about quieter leaders, we're not burdened by the "liability of charisma," which sets up an expectation that we'll be dynamos behind the microphone. It's important to elevate our energy so that we capture and keep the attention of the people in the room. That doesn't mean we have to turn it on, Tony Robbins–style. It does mean that we need to rest up, be prepared, and project more energy than we may be used to in order to have a strong stage presence. Your energy will come from being passionate about your topic, being prepared and confident, and having a compelling desire to share your message. You might even find that it's one of those rare times you actually get energy from other people. Unlike blogging or social media, you're looking people in the eye and seeing smiles, hearing laughter, and experiencing the impact of your words, up close and personal. This kind of real-time affirmation (at least, we hope it's affirmation, and they're laughing with you, not at you!) keeps you going and energizes your voice and presence.

In considering how public speaking may or may not fit into your business model, look at the norms in your own particular industry. If your peers and role models include public speaking in their business development activities, you should seriously consider joining them. While the speaker circuit is filled with coaches, consultants, financial planners, and others who have service-based businesses, there's plenty of room for product-based businesses. You have wisdom to share, whether it's about lessons learned, goal setting, growth and collaboration, planning, and managing employees, vendors, and contractors.

How Does Public Speaking Build Your Tribe (and by Extension, Your Business)?

One major reason I love public speaking is that it helps me reach a larger number of people with a single burst of energy. Preparing for a speaking engagement is done mostly in private, and if I'm taking care of myself, I'm sure not to schedule anything after the event. That just leaves the event itself for which I need to turn my energy more outward. I only need to extrovert for a little while, on one day, for an hour or two.

If you want more evidence that public speaking and presenting might be advantageous, consider this: When asked what their biggest fears were, people ranked public speaking higher than death. Death! While that might be an exaggeration, there is anecdotal truth that more people would rather get a root canal without anesthesia than give a speech. This gives you a golden opportunity to step up and stand out while being (relatively) in control. Over the years I've met many introverts who actually enjoy public speaking, and it results in increased business for them. If you can cultivate a comfort for it, you will stand out.

Scott Berkun is an introvert, author of *Confessions of a Public Speaker*, and professional speaker. I'll never forget something he shared during a presentation I attended several years ago: *We are all public speakers.* Any time we open our mouths and say something to someone else, we are speaking in public. And most of the time, we're speaking without preparation or much time to think. So in many ways, you're already well on your way to being a public speaking pro!

If publishing a book or creating information products is part of your business plan, public speaking is an absolute necessity. Before you write the book or create the product, you are establishing your reputation, gathering feedback and testimonials, and fine-tuning your message. You are also compiling evidence that an agent or publisher needs in order to gauge whether or not there's an audience for your message. After publication or distribution, speaking becomes a vehicle for sales. Depending on the type of book or product you have, it might even make your speaking more lucrative, allowing you to do fewer, higher-paying engagements for more select audiences.

While it might seem counterintuitive to say this about an activity most people fear worse than death, it's true: Getting up in front of audiences and sharing your message builds confidence. UK musician and introvert blogger Andy Mort has learned that sheer repetition is one key to increasing confidence. He says, "The more experiences I've had, the bigger bank of experiences I have to draw on and know that everything's going to be just fine."

Each time you get up there without dying, fainting, freezing, or hyperventilating, you've succeeded. You'll know deeper and deeper in your being that you have the capacity to inspire others and engage people with your business.

The audience wants you to succeed. It is (thankfully) rare to encounter an audience that is hostile or unreceptive to what you have to say. Our imaginations can work overtime and make us paranoid. Someone looking at their smartphone becomes a text message to their friend, sharing how terrible you are. Two people whispering and laughing quietly at their table becomes a critique of your attempt at humor. Instead of paranoia, go into the situation from a place of "pronoia"; believe that the world is conspiring *for* you. The audience is rooting for you and sending you positive energy. While it doesn't always make the butterflies go away, it does help to remember that the audience is on your side.

People who appear natural and relaxed behind the microphone weren't born that way. They achieved their level of comfort after making (and witnessing) dozens of boring, mediocre, and nerve-wracking presentations, each time learning how to improve and building their confidence.

When Susan Cain, author of *Quiet: The Power of Introverts in a World That Can't Stop Talking* and cofounder of the Quiet Revolution, was booked to do a TED talk to coincide with her book's publication, she embarked on what she called her "Year of Speaking Dangerously." She joined Toastmasters, hired coaches, and did extensive preparation. It doesn't have to be something as big as a TED talk to call for similar measures.

The first step is to normalize the activity by hanging around people who have what you want. There is certainly value in spending time with peers who are in the same stage as you (defining, searching, practicing). There is also great value in networking with and learning from people who have achieved what you want to achieve. It normalizes the goal. When you're around someone who has become an in-demand speaker, written a book, and runs a successful business, you are reminded that you, too, can do—will do—those things. Those people might be formal mentors or someone you have coffee with every month. Over time, their achievements, ideas, energy, and experience will virtually rearrange your neurons. They once were where you are, and one day you will be where they are. It's a process. It moves forward one action, one belief, and one connection at a time.

And then it will happen. You'll be listening to someone give a presentation and the thought will cross your mind, "I could do that. Not only could I, I want to!" That might be the turn of the key that revs your engine. Before you lose your nerve (it happens!), drive that engine right over to your closest Toastmasters club. It's among the safest, most affirming places to become more comfortable with your speaking skills. Once you feel you're ready, branch out to new audiences (besides your spouse and pets). There is almost no shortage of places that need speakers. An easy place to start is service clubs, such as your local Rotary, Exchange, and Kiwanis groups. Then you can move into more professionally oriented organizations that are more likely to contain your ideal audience. Formal networking groups, industry-specific associations, and entrepreneurial service groups and forums are a logical next step.

Business communication coach and author of *Self-Promotion for Introverts* Nancy Ancowitz offers us this encouragement: "Take stretch assignments that answer the question, 'Where can I speak that will help a certain community and give myself the opportunity to build this muscle?' Do it every day, do it in front of people, and buddy up with people who will help you. So you can practice your skills, they can practice theirs, and you'll make each other better."

As you become more comfortable, explore the possibilities for corporate and nonprofit speaking engagements. Corporations and larger nonprofits often have professional development series for their employees, seminars for clients, and opportunities to speak at conferences or larger events. As soon as you decide you're interested in pursuing those types of engagements, begin collecting testimonials and positioning yourself to be introduced to the influencers in the company. These are often the human resource or marketing executives. However, any connection in a company is potentially a foot in the door.

I spoke at a professional administrators association daylong conference, and one of the attendees was an assistant to an executive at Starbucks headquarters. She kindly passed my name along to the coordinator for their personal development series, and I was subsequently booked to give a presentation to sixty Starbucks partners. I'm grateful that this referral occurred early in my business. I learned the valuable lesson that you never know where the next opportunity is going to surface.

Finally, I want to acknowledge that while we technically know what to do, it can still be stressful. As introverts, we're aware that an activity like public speaking is, well, public. We are stretched into telling our story in a way that opens us up to scrutiny and heightens our vulnerability. It's not that extroverts have an easy time; it's simply that the act of talking things out in front of people comes more naturally to them.

My earliest experiences with public speaking were very scripted. I literally wrote my talk out, word for word. I didn't quite trust that what was going to come out of my mouth wouldn't be complete gibberish. I didn't have complete confidence that I could keep my train of thought going, or that if I got off track I could get back on again. But now, I no longer need a script, in large part because I've had years of practice. I've taken steps to build my confidence: videotaping myself, being part of a mastermind group focused on public speaking, enlisting people I trust to attend my presentations and provide honest feedback. And one of the most powerful tools in my toolbox might also be one of the most unexpected: improv.

How to Ditch the Script

When I took a speech class in college, I learned a new word that I loved to say: extemporaneous. I loved to say it, and what it meant scared me to death.

To be extemporaneous means to ad-lib—to speak (and presumably, to speak intelligently) without a chance to prepare, at the drop of a hat. Another *Merriam-Webster* definition says, "happening suddenly and often unexpectedly and usually without clearly known causes or relationships."

To some introverts, that's the very definition of a nightmare.

As we explored in Chapter 1, the primary way we define introversion is where we get our energy (from solitude and quiet time). A close runner-up to that is how we process information. Introverts are internal processors. While extroverts do more external, verbal processing of their thoughts and ideas, we introverts take in a piece of information and think it over silently or on paper until it feels ready to be shared.

And that's why the lovely and loaded word *extemporaneous* can be a potential stumbling block.

Our ability to think deeply and thoroughly is truly an asset. I wouldn't trade it for anything. It makes me, me. That said, it's important to recognize that we live in a culture that values being quick on our feet. There's not always time or space to look before we leap (at least, not to look the ten times that we'd like to!).

The more chance there is of stubbing your toe, the more chance you have of stepping into success.

—Anonymous

I knew for some time that my discomfort with being put on the spot could end up as a liability if I didn't find a way to cultivate some spontaneity. When it comes to speaking up in groups or grabbing the bull by the horns, introverts can still be thinking about what they want to say or do while others have already chimed in and moved on.

One of the first phone calls I made when I decided to dedicate my work to the mighty introvert was to my friend Leif. Leif is an extrovert who asks you to make up a story when you leave a message on his voice mail. He's really brilliant, and I wanted to create an "Improv for Introverts" workshop experience to address exactly the fear I had.

What I learned—and what the introverts who joined us learned—has helped make being extemporaneous not quite as scary. We were reminded that life itself is extemporaneous; after all, we don't wake up every morning with the day's script waiting for us in our email inbox. The moments during the workshop when we felt the most stressed were the ones when we were in our heads too much. Once we let go of overthinking and always trying to be prepared for what *might* happen, we relaxed and had fun. The parallels to how we approach everyday life are not hard to see!

Here are some parting thoughts on speaking, all drawn from

the lessons of improv, that I hope will give you a fresh perspective on how to approach public speaking:

Ditch perfection. When we're flipping things around in our heads, we're often looking for the right answer or response. It has to be just so. Improv asks that you let go of the impulse to try to be perfect. Relax. Be real. Tap into your inner kid who is willing to fall down and get back up a thousand times when trying something new.

Make the leap. Introverts sometimes like to stand at the edge and watch how others do something before jumping into the fire. This can translate to others seeing introverts as followers rather than leaders. Opportunity doesn't always wait for us to scope things out. Because improv is a safe space to ditch perfection, it's also a safe space to practice leaping before we look.

Tell the truth. Life's not about making stuff up or being something you're not; neither is improv. Some of the cleverest, funniest, and most touching moments happen when someone boldly speaks the truth. If we set the intention to "call it like we see it," then the pressure to "be creative" is released. And as Scott Berkun writes, "The easiest way to be interesting is to be honest. People rarely say what they truly feel, yet this is what audiences desire most."[1]

Say yes. There are few things that shut down a conversation or a good time faster than the word *no*. The same holds true in improv. It's all about accepting someone's offer. "Yes, and" keeps up the momentum and positive energy.

Don't try to be funny. One thing people assume about improv is that it's all about being funny. After all, what about people like Johnny Carson, Dave Letterman, Steve Martin, and Jerry Seinfeld? Good news: They are all extemporaneous introverts! And do they ever look like they're *trying* to be funny? My guess is that they end up that way because they say yes, call it like they see it, make the leap, and allow things to be messy.

Accelerate failure. Once we accept that we are going to fail on our way to success, it's easier to learn from it. Learning from failure (rather than avoiding it or giving up when it happens) transforms it. Rather than seeing something as a mistake, you have an opportunity to view it as an "interesting choice."

> *Living at risk is jumping off the cliff and building your wings on the way down.* —Ray Bradbury

The Key to Community

We've covered a range of ways to build and engage your tribe, including social media, blogging, and public speaking. They're all powerful methods, each leveraging introvert strengths in a particular way. But if we're not intentional, we can tie ourselves up in knots about the dos and don'ts of building community. We can overcomplicate our approach and lose sight of our core objective. According to artist and author Mary Anne Radmacher, it comes down to something very simple: "Be authentic. If the purpose of the community is to sell something that you use, then disclose that.

Be transparent. Don't sneak in veiled references to the product that you're selling. If you're selling, sell it, own it, be true to what you're trying to achieve; and if you simply want to create a conversation, then start the conversation and invite people."

Introvert Entrepreneur Focus

Chris Guillebeau, founder of World Domination Summit and author of *The Art of Non-Conformity*, *The $100 Startup*, and *The Happiness of Pursuit*

You've built a number of tribes, including nonconformists and world dominators. I've experienced the World Domination Summit, and I was blown away by the sense of community. What did you and your team do to create that feeling?

We tried to be sensitive. The first thing was being aware that there were a lot of different people from different backgrounds coming, and we wanted to be cognizant of that fact. We also wanted to deliberately encourage participation from people who were introverts or highly sensitive, because they wouldn't normally come to a conference with three thousand people. We tried, as much as possible, to market to them and let them know that they would feel welcome.

A lot of it is finding the right people in terms of the event staff, the volunteers, and then of course the attendees themselves. So much of the magic of something like that is really making sure that the right people are there. Then we try to honor the people who are part of it; we try to recognize them as much as possible.

Communities come in all shapes and sizes, and it doesn't seem to matter if we've put ourselves in front of three people or three thousand, most introverts find the entire experience tiring. What advice do you have based on your own experiences of balancing your energy?

It all sounds overwhelming, but that's not how it started. I began doing meet-ups with maybe about five people. I went on this book tour years ago, and I went to all fifty states. Some of those stops were in really small areas; they had around five or ten people, and at the time that was really big for me, too.

So I do believe that the scale of an experience that you gain, those experiences translate to bigger things later, but it's important to remember, "big" is relative.

I take care of myself mostly afterwards. With an event like the World Domination Summit, it's a very immersive kind of experience. There is really nothing I can do but be present and focused during that time. And when I say "that time" it's not just a three-day event, it's also the lead up and take down. Then I try to go away afterwards. And even if it's a small thing, like if I'm doing a short event, whether it's my own or I'm a part of someone else's, it still takes a lot out of me, so I plan for later to be on my own.

The bigger the dream or the tribe, the more introverts could start to fear that all the people and expectations will suck the life out of them. What advice would you have about keeping it all in perspective?

I think if you have a big dream, you essentially have this calling in your life, and it's like this kernel of inspiration. I tend to think, "How could that possibly suck the life out of me? An inspiration like that for me is going to bring life, it's going to bring joy." It might intimidate you a little bit, you might be a little bit afraid or anxious about it, but that doesn't mean it's going to suck the life out of you; in fact, it's probably the opposite.

You should chase those dreams. You shouldn't run away from them or hide. I feel like whatever negative experience you're going to have is going to come from failing to pursue that dream. If you have this dream and you don't do it, you're really going to regret that later.

Chapter 7

When Two Heads Are Better Than One

Collaboration: Why Bother?

> *I don't believe anything really revolutionary has ever been invented by committee . . . I'm going to give you some advice that might be hard to take. That advice is: Work alone . . . Not on a committee. Not on a team.*
>
> —Steve Wozniak

Steve Wozniak's words are music to an introvert's ears, and it's no surprise they were spoken by a well-known introvert. They give us permission to fly solo. Business-by-committee approaches can slow progress and muck up the works. There are communication challenges, conflicting agendas, and unexpected demands on our precious time and energy.

In my own case, my independence and curiosity has led me to develop what my husband refers to as a "Swiss Army knife" quality.

Whatever the situation, I have the knife, nail file, corkscrew, tweezers, or scissors to solve it. If I can start with a tool already in my toolbox, I will. It's a valuable entrepreneurial asset that has served me well. It's saved me money, time, and relationships. After all, bringing in additional people means I have to think about and deal with their needs, challenges, bright ideas, fears, and egos.

Introverts and independence go hand in hand. It doesn't mean that other people aren't important to us; we simply are more deliberate (and even cautious) about who we invite into our inner world. We see it very simply: people in = energy out. We can absolutely love and adore those people, and they can still exhaust us.

I've noticed that just as I'm protective of my energy when it comes to personal relationships, I'm almost more protective when it comes to who I bring into my entrepreneurial life. My Swiss Army knife mentality allowed me to be a one-woman show for a while. What I didn't know, I could figure out. Until . . .

Until I couldn't figure it out anymore. Until I hit the wall of "OK, I've tried everything I can think of—now what?" That's when I realized that some things were too big to tackle on my own and that for the ambitious dreams I had, two heads were better than one.

It's a common theme among introvert entrepreneurs. Like the old cliché about men refusing to ask for directions, we'll sometimes do *anything* to find a solution except ask another person for help.

Whenever we bring someone else into our psyche and make the internal external, we are acutely aware of our vulnerability. We are exposed. It means there's at least one more person in the world who expects something from us and from whom we expect something. That alone is enough to make us stick it out solo longer than might be wise.

How do we introverts move through the discomfort of vulnerability in service to our business? And how do we invite others into our work in a way that doesn't zap our energy?

When It's Time to Consider Collaboration

As an introvert entrepreneur, you probably have a fairly strong independent streak and may even take pride in considering yourself a jack- or jill-of-all-trades.

When that pride is part of our identity, it's easy to make the mistake of waiting until we're practically in crisis before considering a collaborative solution. There are a few business markers that might indicate it would be a good time to rally some troops:

You've reached your expertise ceiling. There may come a point when you receive a request from a client or customer or have a fabulous idea that's beyond your scope of knowledge.

You want to reach new markets. What if you decide that you're ready to get your message out to a new group of potential clients or customers? It's easy to become market myopic when you're operating in a silo.

You're craving the possibilities of collective brainpower. Even for solitude-loving introverts, it can be refreshing to find a thought partner with whom you can brainstorm ideas and connect disparate dots. A bonus to involving someone else in your process: The right person can help you to break out of any hamster-wheel thoughts you might be having about a particular challenge or opportunity.

You're secure in your business and ready to expand. You're coming from a place of power and success and ready to reach out to others. The right kind of collaboration will serve to complement what you have to offer, not dilute it.

The decision to involve another person in your business is not one to take lightly. It can be a bit intimidating because you're entering into new agreements and even developing a new vocabulary to explain how you operate your business. There are a lot of details to discuss, expectations to clarify, and the need to come to a common understanding about how you're going to work together. Not only that but each person in the collaboration is bringing his or her own biases, experiences, beliefs, fears, and strengths to the table.

With something this potentially complex, it's critical for the introvert entrepreneur to apply due diligence to the situation. This is not only true for any legal or formal aspects of the partnership; it's also true of the assessment of mutual readiness to enter into a partnership and how well you and your partner(s) are energetically matched. Without due diligence, you risk not only your business but your sanity.

When you're ready, you can approach the other person casually. A short script provided by business coach Felicia Lee suggests this for introverts, "I love what you do. I think that we should have a conversation and talk about how we can build business together. If you're interested, what does your time look like in a couple of weeks? Let's have coffee and just get to know each other." If that doesn't work for you, vary the text so that it reflects your style and personality. Or ask a colleague who has reached out in a similar way if you can have a copy of the email (identifying details removed) so you can get ideas about what to say.

The Different Faces of Collaboration

*I never did anything alone. Whatever was accomplished in
this country was accomplished collectively.*

—Golda Meir

For our purposes, we're going to focus on informal partnerships
that don't require legal agreements (learn more in the Resources
section of TheIntrovertEntrepreneur.com). There are numerous ways
you can expand your business by widening your circle of resources,
support, and influence.

Coaching Isn't Just for Athletes

One of the first partnerships many business owners enter into is to
hire a personal coach. Just like a coach for a sports team, a personal
coach can help you find the right moves to make the play, but she
won't make the play itself. A coach—whether it's someone who
focuses exclusively on your business or someone who does a hybrid
of personal and entrepreneur coaching—can become an invaluable
part of your team, offering an outside perspective as well as drawing on experiences from working with different types of clients and
business models.

Coaching is usually a one-on-one partnership that involves a
professional (preferably certified) coach and you as the client. You
and your coach talk on a regular basis, anywhere from one to four
times per month. You set the agenda and determine the priorities,
and it's the coach's responsibility to guide you through your agenda
so that you reach your desired outcomes. This is done through

listening carefully to what you're saying (and not saying), being able to see the big picture and bring you back to your originally stated goals and values, and helping you hold yourself accountable for actions you have chosen.

You should be able to bring just about any challenge or opportunity to your coach. She doesn't have to be an expert in your niche or particular business—my clients have ranged from an information technology specialist to a science curriculum writer to a structural engineer. I have no experience in any of those areas, but I do have experience in creating and implementing business strategies that introverts find effective in growing their businesses. My expertise lies in the *process and strategies* involved in entrepreneurship.

The same should be true for your coach. He should be an expert in coaching: asking insightful questions, reflecting back what he sees in you, challenging your assumptions, reframing counterproductive stories, and holding a space that allows you to process through your thoughts in an intentional, forward-moving manner. As an introvert, you will probably want a coach who leaves plenty of space in the conversation, so you can process on your own time. You also want someone who will help you find ways of doing the extroverted business activities while honoring your introversion.

Coaches vary in their approach to the partnership, depending on your needs and their style. I've been with my own coach for more than four years, and as long as I continue to receive value from the relationship, I'll keep it going. (By the way, your coach doesn't necessarily have to be an introvert himself; different energies bring different perspectives!) It's possible you could accomplish your objectives in a few months or a year. And there are even cases when two or three "power sessions" will do the trick. A good coach will help you figure out what time frame works best for your particular situation. My experience with introverts is that we appreciate time to process and try things out, both mentally and in practice. Don't allow impatience to rush the relationship; meaningful progress takes time.

Coaches differ from consultants; they don't give you direct advice, and they don't tell you what to do. Instead, they are trained to support your own self-discovery. If you are feeling insecure, afraid, overwhelmed, or stuck, the right coach will help you move through those challenges.

Hiring a Consultant

Some situations call for the more hands-on, directive approach of the consultant. Unlike coaches, consultants advise you on what to do. Some consultants will look at every aspect of your business and advise you on strategies, potential obstacles, and opportunities. Others have specific content-area expertise, such as marketing, social media, licensing, and expansion. If it's important to you that the consultant speaks your industry-specific language, it might be advantageous to hire a consultant who has experience with your particular business or has provided similar services to yours in the past.

There's one thing that both a coach and a consultant bring to the table: accountability. We introverts have the potential to become too self-reliant and not make ourselves vulnerable to others, especially when it comes to our ambitions and dreams. They are highly personal, too precious to share. So they remain inside us, and no one else knows if we're making them come to life or not. A good consultant or coach will help you create a solid business plan and design benchmarks to hold you accountable. This dramatically increases your effectiveness and follow-through. Yes, it makes you vulnerable. But the payoff is that you've expanded your brainpower by at least two, and you have an advocate who is committed to helping you succeed.

Accountability Partners

What if you're not ready for a coach or consultant? The next best thing is having a trusted, reliable accountability partner. An accountability partner is another entrepreneur, preferably someone not in the same industry or target market as you. The basic purpose is to share goals with one another—either on a daily or weekly basis—and commit to accomplishing them within a certain time frame. You email or call one another to share your goals, then agree on when you will reconnect to report back.

Besides providing focus, connection, and motivation, there are numerous benefits to having an accountability partner, especially if you tend to be a work-alone introvert.

> **Structure.** There are certain business tasks and ideas that no one knows about but you, so they can continue to be recycled on the to-do list. Having regular accountability conversations gives you a structure and deadlines for those projects so you can move forward instead of spinning and thinking, "Well, nobody knows about it, so it doesn't have to happen today . . ."

> **Feedback.** Over time, your partner will know almost as much about your business as you do, and vice versa. That makes it possible to provide solicited feedback about what each of you notices about the other person's priorities and strategies.

> **Problem solving.** Whether it's negotiating with a new client, making a prospecting call, or dealing with a sticky situation,

you become a sounding board for each other and can offer direct, informed advice based on your intimate knowledge of one another's business and goals.

Acknowledgment and encouragement. As your partnership matures, you'll start to see the long arc of your progress and be able to remind each other of how well we're doing, especially when one of you gets discouraged or loses focus.

Advisory Boards

If you want more people involved, consider putting together an advisory board. It doesn't seem very introvert-like, I know. But it's a low-risk way to gather a variety of opinions and create a cadre of champions for you and your business.

Your advisory board doesn't have to meet like a traditional board does (although it might be a nice opportunity to connect people with one another and strengthen your alliances). You can consider them a group but consult with them one-on-one by phone, email, or in person. Find the most efficient and effective means of communication that you can keep consistent. The board can be made up of people who you admire and those who are a few steps ahead of you on the entrepreneurial path. You can include mentors, former teachers or employers, or someone in your industry who focuses on a different market (and therefore isn't a direct competitor).

Beyond these more informal affiliations, you may want to collaborate with colleagues by hiring them as independent contractors or for short- or long-term project-based work. The information shared here applies to those types of relationships, in addition to casual ones. The only substantial difference between the two is that when you're hiring or contracting with someone, the financial and legal considerations are essential parts of the agreements you make together.

Who Do You Want Aboard?

Once you've determined the timing is right to partner, and you are clear on the type of partnership needed, you're ready to consider specifically who will be your partner. In fact, the desire to partner might precede knowing exactly what the partnership will entail; you may just know that more brainpower is needed to move forward or you may have a strong feeling about wanting to work with a particular person. This question of who is especially critical for introverts because social interaction drains our energy. You need to choose collaborators who return at least as much energy to your enterprise as they take.

This is why it's important to be clear about with whom you want to work and to whom you're going to say no. We may be tempted to open ourselves up to anyone who wants to work with us. It's not easy to say no. Sometimes a potential partner seems to fit when it comes to achieving a similar goal . . . yet, there's not that click you feel when you're connected with your ideal partner. Even worse, there are the relationships that, for no reason you can put your finger on, just *grate*. Pay attention to this and trust your gut. Your business is too important and your energy too precious to be sidetracked by relationships that feel out of sync.

Assuming you've figured out the why and what of a partnership, how will you determine the who? Consider those within your network who you admire and feel a connection with. Who energizes you? Here are a few traits you want to consider:

Complementary skills. Someone who is highly skilled at navigating social media might be a good fit for you if you prefer more traditional communication methods.

Complementary energy. You can tell a lot about how well matched you are energetically by the way you feel before, during, and after conversations. Anxiety, dread, or exhaustion before, during, or after an interaction is a red flag. You're looking for a sense of warmth, inspiration, and positive energy.

Easy conversation. Regardless if your potential partner is an introvert or extrovert, notice the following as you interact:

Do you feel like the conversation is two-way or one-way?

Are you able to finish sharing your thoughts or is there a sense of starting and stopping with lots of half-finished sentences?

Does the other person ask you questions, then leave time for you to answer?

Are you comfortable with occasional stretches of silence when working together?

Do you feel heard by the other person? Does he or she demonstrate active listening skills?

More respect than love. Here's what I learned toward the end of my classical music training: I love music too much to be a musician. Similarly, you may love your colleague too much to be formal collaborators. You can find lots of people to format your newsletter or manage your website, but there are only a few people who can fill the role of a trusted friend. Think twice before jeopardizing a prized personal relationship.

Six Partnership Pitfalls

People—especially introverts—sometimes avoid or dismiss collaboration because they see it as more trouble than it's worth. One of their own may have fallen apart or even destroyed a relationship with a colleague. While there's no guarantee or foolproof formula, there are steps you can take to decrease your chances of a calamitous collaboration.

It's critical that the partnership be built on a solid foundation of shared trust, respect, and expectations. When you're first forming the partnership, you might get caught up in the excitement of new ideas and figure all of the details will take care of themselves. Sometimes we luck out. The terms of the collaboration are simple and obvious, not complicated by anything financial, legal, or proprietary. Often, though, each party has a meaningful, tangible stake in the outcome—and that's where the devil might be lurking in the details. Here are some things that can jeopardize even the most well-meaning partnership.

Making Assumptions

Relationships in general—and professional collaborations in particular—are susceptible to falling victim to assumptions on the part of one or both people. It's dangerous to enter into the work making assumptions about who is responsible for what and when and how the proceeds will be divided (or not). We must be willing to ask pointed, clarifying questions from the beginning: What are we each accountable for? How often will we meet? How long will this partnership last? Who's going to manage the finances? Who owns the intellectual property we produce? Which resources (including contacts) from our respective businesses can be used for this project?

One more thing to consider: Author Susan Cain shares this about the silent bargains that can happen in a relationship: "We can fall into the trap of thinking, 'OK, I made a concession today, and my strategic partner will remember that six months from now and do the same thing for me six months down the road.'" Cain adds, "And that may be true . . . you hope that it's recorded in a golden book of values. But it's not always true. People often don't really remember the value of the concession you've given. So, a good thing to practice is to say that, if you make a concession today, you think about what concession you can ask for in return on that same day."

Not Talking About the Tough Stuff

Not talking about the tough stuff is closely related to making assumptions. We often make assumptions to avoid talking about difficult issues. A few of the things you might be tempted to gloss over: how money will be handled, who owns the results of your work, whether one person bears more risk or responsibility than the other, and what your exit strategy is if one or both of the parties needs to end the partnership. If there is any aspect of the collaboration that has financial, legal, confidentiality, or intellectual property ramifications, talk it over thoroughly. Seek the advice of professionals as needed. It might be uncomfortable, and it might cost you a little to get assistance, but the expense of not working out those details may be much, much higher.

In addition, being clear about exclusivity is critically important to the partnership. Talk about if either of you is going to be "dating" anyone else during the collaboration. This is also a way to ensure your energy is being used wisely. It can be disconcerting—and trust eroding—when a partner brings a new player to the table without consulting the other partner. Confirm early on who the partners are and whether a few projects on the side are acceptable.

The tough stuff extends to the personal terrain as well. As Cate Brubaker, founder of Small Planet Studio, says, "If it's going to be a long-term collaboration, I think about what might get on my nerves about my collaborator's work style, or if they have quirks that I might have difficulty overlooking. I ask myself honestly if there's the potential that they'll become deal breakers. Of course, I can't foresee everything, so I often rely on my intuition." If you want a collaboration to succeed, it's important that each person feels safe being able to tactfully call attention to personal foibles that interfere with work, in the spirit of creating a productive relationship.

One or All Partners Coming from Fear or Weakness

Ideally, both of the partners should be coming from a place of strength. Each person should feel confident that both businesses are stable, cash flow is predictable and adequate, there is a steady supply and demand for your products and services, and there are no immediate threats that could undermine your position. Make sure that you yourself feel emotionally connected to your work and fully committed to your business. This doesn't mean that you don't experience fleeting doubts, fears, or anxiety. However, when you're working with someone else, you should be at the point where you're able to draw on your introvert strengths of self-awareness and reflection in order to sort through and manage those feelings.

Conversely, be wary if either you or the other person is proposing collaboration because the business is on thin ice. This is the equivalent to having a baby in order to save a marriage. Remember the old adage: "Wherever you go, there you are" (attributed online to many sources, from Confucius to Thomas à Kempis to the movie *Austin Powers, The Spy Who Shagged Me*). You will be the same person in a partnership as you are out of it. A person who is operating from a scarcity mindset will not suddenly become optimistic when paired with a stronger person in a high-stakes situation.

Roles and Responsibilities Are Not Clear

Have you ever seen that brilliant skit from Abbott and Costello, "Who's on First?" If not, find it online. The two men banter back and forth and talk in circles about a baseball game, not understanding each other in the slightest. Abbott thinks he's being crystal clear about the names of the players, and Costello thinks he's being deliberately evasive.

This comedy routine could easily play out in real life if roles and responsibilities aren't clarified early in a collaboration. If at every juncture, you have to ask yourselves, "Now, who's on first? What's on second?" you'll both end up frustrated and definitely not laughing. Talk about your respective strengths and challenges and what they mean to the work involved. For instance, as an introvert, you might relish the behind-the-scenes work and want to dig into it with enthusiasm. Putting up posters all over town or calling the media to pitch a story might not be your cup of tea. But in the spirit of no assumptions, talk about it; you may, in fact, *want* to do them, either because you actually enjoy them, are good at them, or feel like you want the practice. Don't leave who's on first and what's on second to chance.

Conflicting Expectations

Conflicting expectations have the potential to be one of the more heartbreaking outcomes of collaboration. The project is finished, and one partner is pleased with the outcome, and the other is disappointed. "We made money!" one person says, while the other reflects, "But we didn't generate any new leads." This unfortunate situation can lead to not just stress and miscommunication but the untimely dissolution of the partnership.

The solution is simple and easily addressed from the beginning: Discuss and agree on shared expectations and definitions of success. What is the ultimate purpose of the project? If you come away with only one thing, what will it be? How will you know it's been successful? Are there measurable outcomes you want to define? How will you measure the less tangible outcomes, if they are important to you? You don't want to put in an enormous amount of time, energy, and resources only to find out that you were each expecting a different result. Or worse, one person was deeply invested in a particular outcome and the other was viewing it all as a grand experiment. It would be extremely disheartening to the invested individual if goals weren't met and his frustration was answered with, "Well, but look at how much we learned!"

Conflict Avoidance

Of all of these pitfalls, conflict avoidance is perhaps the most potentially damaging. No one likes conflict and confrontation, and some introverts will go to great lengths to avoid it. It's not so much that we're shy about speaking our minds or can't handle conflict. We simply know the process will require a high expenditure of personal energy.

If a disagreement occurs, your first impulse might be to stuff your feelings and withdraw. Or perhaps you elect to write an email or otherwise find a way to forgo face-to-face communication. However, when a valuable partnership is in jeopardy, nothing can take the place of direct dialogue.

Consider reframing it less as conflict or confrontation (which are words loaded with negative connotations) and more as a conversation. You are simply sharing concerns before things escalate to full-blown drama or a complete meltdown. To prepare yourself for the conversation, reflect on these questions:

- How would I want someone to deliver this news to me?
- What would be the best possible outcome from the conversation?
- What's the worst that could happen?
- What is the empathetic yet professional response to the worst-case scenario?
- Knowing that I can't take care of my colleague, make it all better, or control how she feels about this, what *do* I have control over?
- What might she be afraid of, and how can I leave space for that fear to be expressed?

This series of inquiries leads you through a process of checking in on your own feelings and motivations as well as walking a mile in the other person's shoes. As introverts, we tend to forget that other people can't read our minds. These questions give us a framework to take internal thoughts and feelings and turn them into conversation points.

Six Best Practices of Highly Effective Collaborations

Just as there are clear don'ts associated with collaboration, there are definite dos that contribute to an energizing relationship for everyone involved. Nothing can be taken for granted. A partnership between two introverts doesn't mean you're going to instantly understand one another and never have issues. Nor does pairing up with an extrovert mean automatic craziness. Either partnership combination can result in success or misery. What will make the difference is the degree to which you adhere to some best practices. The presence of these behaviors is an indicator that you're heading in the right direction. They don't guarantee a successful outcome, but they do contribute to having a more satisfying partnership experience.

Engaging in Open, Frequent Communication

Establish consistent communication, whether it's by email, phone, or in person. You can call them check-ins or process checks, whatever seems appropriate to your work. Of course, there will be situation-specific communication that happens outside of set times, but those discussions are usually limited to the scope of the issue at hand. They aren't designed for addressing bigger-picture concerns, opportunities, or questions that come up as a project progresses.

Having a set structure for regular check-ins is advantageous for the partnership and especially for you as an introvert. Preparation time allows you to think through what you're going to say, which is particularly important if you need to share something that's sensitive or emotional. The check-in meetings give you a safe, ready-made place to do that and allow everyone to take the pulse of the collaboration and make sure things are going smoothly.

Identifying and Challenging Assumptions

There's an old saying that "to assume makes an ass out of you and me." Yet, despite this, we make assumptions all the time, even without being aware of it. So it's highly probable that without due diligence and vigilance, assumptions will creep into our collaborations.

Personal assumptions are ingrained in our consciousness, long before we started our businesses. Coaches often refer to these assumptions as "stories." Your story is a set of beliefs that you're carrying around about what you are and aren't capable of doing. For introverts, these stories sometimes directly contradict what you know you need to do to be successful. Here are a few that I've both heard and experienced: "I'm not good at networking." "I wouldn't be good at sales." "I don't think people find me interesting; they don't understand me." "I am too quiet to be a successful entrepreneur." "You have to be extroverted to make a lot of money."

Every last one of these statements is a story. It's an idea that's been planted in our heads and perpetuated by parents, friends, teachers, and colleagues. Or we came to those conclusions on our own after one failed or awkward experience. Whatever their origin or basis, we need to thoroughly vet and come to terms with them. Otherwise, we will inevitably carry them into the partnership, where they may manifest in unhealthy ways. Challenge the assumptions, and allow your partner to do the same. In a trusting and respectful collaboration, you'll be able to shine the light on those stories and sort through them so that they don't become an obstacle to your mutual success.

Professionally, it's critical to identify any assumptions related to the who, what, when, where, and why of the collaboration. Introvert entrepreneurs are creative and thorough and might have fleshed out every detail and action before even consulting a partner. That can potentially lead to blanks in the conversation that are never filled in out loud, only in the introvert's head. As with so many other instances, the internal needs to be made external. Effective partnerships are based on clear role definition, with each person being 100 percent certain about his or her responsibilities.

Assumptions about who will do what should be examined. If your collaborator knows you're a writer and assumes that you'll take on all of the content creation for the project, he might not know that you really want to try your hand at designing the website. You'd have to have a baseline of knowledge or skill in order to do that, of course, but he might not know if he doesn't ask you and you don't tell him. If you're working together for the first time, and your people-pleaser side kicks in, you might not contradict him when he says, "You're such a great writer, you'll take care of that part, right?" His assumption becomes your reality, and you could end up feeling increasingly resentful of your assigned responsibility. If you adopt a no-assumptions rule for working together and commit to voicing your feelings, you at least have an opportunity to explore other options. Then it's about a choice you're making and agreeing on together rather than an assignment.

Sharing Expectations and Definitions of Success

As Peter Drucker remarked, "What gets measured gets done." Successful collaborations have clearly defined measurements of success. The core metrics—financial, reach, engagement, growth, quality—should be outlined and agreed on. Others, such as strengthening a particular skill or making meaningful connections with new people, might be harder to measure but are no less important to articulate. You don't have to share every expectation; the more critical point is that you're each aware of the other's expectations and its level of importance to the partnership. Then you can have open communication about how things are proceeding and whether each person's needs (professional or personal) are being met.

Being Equally Invested in the Work

It might go without saying, but no assumptions means no assumptions: All of the partners need to be clear about their commitment to the collaboration from the start. Neither party should ever feel taken advantage of. Each person has to be equally invested, with the same to gain or lose as the other. An exception might be if you know from the beginning that one person might benefit more than the other, and you're both in agreement with that.

In addition, no one has a crystal ball or can predict the circumstances under which a commitment might change. "You want to know that you're generally on the same page," offers Cate Brubaker. "Open and transparent communication throughout the process is almost more important than having all the 'what ifs' worked out in advance."

Coming from Strength

Setting up your partnership for success means that you both believe success is possible. You've each experienced success on your own and are ready to expand your knowledge, reach, or work in ways that will be mutually beneficial to others. There is a sense that $1 + 1 = 3$, because each business has an opportunity to magnify its capacity more than it could on its own.

This doesn't mean everyone is Pollyanna and avoids the difficult conversations. There may be moments of relative weakness or feelings of scarcity. But an effective collaboration has the transparency and resilience to work through them. Feelings of fear or anxiety are addressed directly and compassionately. This is only possible when the people involved are working from a healthy, confident state of being. For introverts, this means trusting our own voice and authority and being able to speak out proactively, when needed.

Having an Exit Strategy

It may be advisable to set a term limit on the partnership from the beginning. If you are an introvert who appreciates structure, this lets you put some boundaries around the arrangement. You can anticipate how you will pace out your work and, therefore, your energy. You can also consider mimicking the lifestyles of the rich and famous and drafting a "prenup" agreement before any financial or legal resources exchange hands. Clearly outline what will happen and how work, clients, customers, information, finances, and so on will be divided in the event of a dissolution, whether planned or unexpected. This one move will save you tremendous stress during a time that's already inherently stressful.

When You're Ready to Reach Out

If you're feeling overwhelmed—or even diffident—at the thought of reaching out to someone, you're not alone. However, don't allow yourself to get stuck in an attraction–avoidance vortex. Instead, consider the following two choices.

Start Small

If you've been flying solo with only informal support from friends, family, or colleagues, start with exploring small ways you can bring more formal relationships into your work. Join or start a regular mastermind group. Partner on a short-term, stand-alone, low-risk project that gives you both a sense of what it would be like to work together (if it's a bust, you can easily extricate yourself). Enlist an accountability partner for mutual support; my twice-weekly phone calls with my accountability partner are critical to my focus and feeling of connection. One of my coaching clients meets regularly with a friend for a two-hour writing block, during which she writes her weekly blog post. Each of these ideas opens up opportunities for you to receive feedback and support, without the potential stress of being dependent on another person for any part of your livelihood.

Be Proactive

Sometimes when we get stressed or depressed about either a particular event or the general direction that things are going, we keep things too close to the vest. We don't open up to our friends and family or share what's going on inside of our heads, even though we trust them more than anyone in the world. Even if someone has been 100 percent supportive of our entrepreneurial risks, we can be loath to reveal our fears, perceived failures, and insecurities. So we suffer in silence.

Don't wait until the plane is going down to reach for an oxygen mask. If you don't reach out for help when you need it, the situation will likely escalate. You'll hit bottom. Alone.

Make a commitment to noticing when a stoic attitude or brave face is keeping you disconnected from support. Try to open up more. Don't wait until you feel so disconnected from everyone that you can't find your way back. Who do you have in your life who can help you decompress the stress in progress? If not a spouse, partner, or friend, consider a coach. Being able to share not only my wins but my losses with my coach has made it easier to let others into my business. Our conversations affirm for me that *I am not alone.*

Introvert Entrepreneur Focus

Mary Anne Radmacher, artist, apronary, and
author of *Courage Doesn't Always Roar*

How did you know it when you were ready to enter into a formal partnership with Applied Insight?

Choosing alliances or partnerships can be tricky business. I've had a handful of circumstances, fully informed upon looking back, that had markers and warnings along the way that I chose to ignore. The difference in my partnership with Applied Insight is that my partnership with Dr. Deanna Davis, the CEO, was tried in several different arenas. We were observers of each other's professional practices, we taught together, I'd read her work. We had tested the waters of a professional relationship in many small ways before agreeing to a more significant affiliation.

What did you learn through the process of doing a successful Kickstarter campaign that would be useful to an introvert entrepreneur considering a similar endeavor?

I was emotionally unprepared for how vulnerable I would feel with such a public "ask" as a Kickstarter campaign. I resisted reading about "how to conduct a successful campaign" and participated full out, from the heart, with my most authentic voice. After thirty years as a public figure it was a roller coaster ride asking for contributions to fulfill a double dream. Deanna and I both reached out to our shared and individual communities. I was overwhelmed with the outpouring of support and affirmation. Still am every time I think about it. And the process that Kickstarter funded is already helping me make a bigger difference in the way I am able to teach and offer processes.

Preparing for a public "ask" or making such a "strong offer," as author Patti Digh likes to call it, requires emotional preparation. I do not usually define myself by much external assessment. That said—there were a few days when the program was inert that my confidence was impacted. That startled me. I would say be prepared with a small support circle (personal systems or people you are inclined to trust) and honor your courage, every day in the process, that you had the guts to declare "I need your help and I am asking."

THE INTROVERT ENTREPRENEUR

What have you found to be the most critical "best practice" that contributes to a successful collaboration?

Narrating process to your partner is important. Partners are not mind readers. If you are too busy to complete a promise, just say that. Silence implies all kinds of things. Don't expect a partner to fill in the blanks of your quiet. Just a quick note, or email acknowledgment, text, or call with a brief update keeps positive momentum up and anxiety and questions down.

Chapter 8

Business Expansion

Bigger and Better, Introvert-Style

Bursting at the Seams: How Do You Know When to Grow?

At some point, your business is going to outgrow the clothes in which it was initially dressed. The clues might come in the form of demand for new or different services from your clients or it might be your gut telling you that it's time to invest in a promising fresh direction.

This is more than having an accountability partner or collaborating on a one-time project as we discussed in the previous chapter. The decision to expand your business by adding full-on partners or staff is one that fundamentally changes how you operate as well as affects your definition of success. What was previously an ambitious goal may now look only adequate. And what was once a risk that you were taking with only your own neck on the line now includes other invested partners, clients, and customers.

How do you know when you're ready? The signs are not unlike

the ones we discussed when we spoke about smaller-scale partnerships. Notice as we review the signs that they are all based in an attitude of abundance; you want to grow because you are successful and your business warrants it. If you decide to expand because something you're doing isn't working or you're afraid if you don't you'll go under, then take a step back and confront the realities of the current situation. Remember: Don't try having a baby to save a marriage. Expanding a troubled business only expands your troubles.

You're ready to consider expansion when:

You've reached your expertise ceiling, but not your vision for the business. There is room for more advancement in services or products, but perhaps the expansion will lead you away from business activities that are your core strengths and into areas where you feel less competent. That's when it's time to call in someone else, so you can stay focused on what you do best.

You want to reach new markets, clients, and customers. Perhaps you've saturated your current market and are ready to expand into a new one. Or you see potential in an area that wasn't available or obvious when you first started your business.

You've decided that you can't do it all by yourself. This is not necessarily because you feel overwhelmed and over-worked, although there might be a touch of that involved. It's more about seeing opportunities and ideas that could come to life if you had a few more hands in the mix. This could be as simple as hiring an administrative assistant or someone part-time to coordinate order fulfillment, marketing, or social media. Who you choose could make or break your efforts, so we'll cover how to create that position so that you have a synergistic match for your introvert energy.

You're ready to stop trading time for money. One of my coaching clients used to base her contract bids on how many hours she estimated a project would take her. She'd add up the hours, multiply them by her hourly rate, and factor in materials and subcontracting costs. From there, she'd have her bid amount. This worked OK and paid the bills, but she never made the amount of money she wanted. Why? Because she wasn't asking for it. She was trading time for money rather than considering how much she wanted to make from a contract or what the contract was worth. She frequently spent more time than she'd estimated, but felt hesitant—or was not able—to bill the client for it. Once she shifted into growth mode and beyond the time-for-money trade-off, she was able to alter her perspective to one that placed an emphasis on her expertise, contribution, and results.

You've achieved a certain amount of success and see that there's still opportunity for growth. Your clients and customers have given you feedback that indicates it's time to move into new areas.

Here's a simple example: You own a bookstore, and your customers are starting to ask if you host book groups. The potential for additional revenue is high because you can offer special deals if everyone in the book group purchases from you, you charge a small fee for using the space, or you offer some other value-added experience that makes your store a book group destination. You know that to do it right, you'll need a coordinator to manage the logistics.

Or perhaps you are a consultant. The volumes of content you've developed have piled up enough that you could create a book, DVDs, or other information products. They would help you reach a larger group of people as well as benefit your current clients. You know those items will take time and special expertise to put together. You can also foresee that it could be an ongoing project, with each presentation turning into a new product. Having a digital media assistant or information products coordinator on your team might be a wise investment.

Notice that I prefaced this list with the words *ready to consider*. You may feel one or more of these statements are true for you, and even then, it's important to weigh the options and understand what's driving you. Your motivation for growth must be based in a belief in what's possible. There should be a sense that you are moving toward something rather than away from something else.

Finding the Pack You'll Lead

Anyone who's worked for someone else has at one time or another thought to themselves, "I could do a better job of managing than this bozo." Well, we might not have been that harsh, but we probably had all the perfect answers and solutions, sitting in our comfortable office out of the line of fire. Finding yourself in the position of "bozo" to others will be an eye-opening experience and potentially challenge your introverted energy. You'll be called on to be more present, more visible, and more verbal than ever before. And you'll discover more personal strengths and challenges than you ever knew you had.

If you've not had much experience in a leadership position be-fore, you may not be aware of your style and how people respond to you in that role. Up until this point, you've been a leader just by virtue of starting your own business. The difference moving forward is that you'll be managing people, not only processes and projects. There's a mind shift that's required when your success or failure changes from affecting only you to involving other people—the stakes are higher.

Numerous things will be different once you bring others into the mix. If you have any issues with control, they will likely be activated almost immediately. You'll become aware of enjoying daily interaction with someone or that you still prefer to have large chunks of time alone. Your style might be conducive to having an employee who needs a strong mentor or you might prefer someone who has more experience and needs less supervision.

The question of your leadership style and how to be an effective leader is too big to address adequately here. There are many leadership characteristics that introverts tend to exhibit; here is a short list, some of which should, by now, have a familiar ring:

- **Thoughtfulness.** Introverts process internally and generally take action only after sufficient consideration. They think before they speak rather than thinking by speaking.
- **Calm, cool, collected.** Because of their thoughtful nature, introverts tend to have a calming energy. This contributes to an atmosphere of trust and safety for others.
- **Aspiration for the company (mission, vision, team), not self.** Being front and center, in the spotlight, is not the typical goal of the introvert. Introverts can and do lead the charge, but the focus is always on the company rather than self-promotion.

- **Takes responsibility as needed, gives credit when it's due.** Their focus on the job at hand means that introverts don't feel a strong need to claim the credit or displace the blame. Do we enjoy recognition? Sure. But it's generally not our primary driver.
- **Active listening skills.** Introverts are keen observers and like to gather information, process it, then come to a conclusion. Most prefer to listen more than talk.
- **Subtle charisma.** Introverted leaders quietly command the respect of those around them and draw people in. Their magnetism is less polarizing and more team oriented.

Note: More leadership resources are recommended in the Resources section of TheIntrovertEntrepreneur.com. Consider reading leadership materials, taking a few workshops or seminars, or engaging a coach to support you in finding your unique style and growing your leadership skills. Even if you remain a solopreneur in the midst of your growth period, you can still be a leader among your peers and within your industry.

Once you've done some introspection about who you are as a leader, it's time to determine who you need to lead. The answer may be obvious. For instance, if you are experiencing a backlog of orders and are having trouble keeping up, an administrative assistant who is responsible for order fulfillment would probably be a wise first hire. You may find there are so many social media and marketing outlets that you could spend all day, every day, just getting the word out. A marketing director or social media assistant would relieve you of that duty and free you up for other business development activities.

In these cases, your task is straightforward: You write a clear job description that includes skills, experience plus education required, responsibilities, evaluation process, expectations, and goals, as appropriate. You might even go so far as to write a detailed portrait of the ideal candidate, including their personality traits and energy levels.

Let's say the type of position you need is less obvious. You simply know that you want more brainpower behind the business. You may be clear about the type of person you want around, even if the particular tasks that person would be performing are still hazy. You might even have a particular person in mind. That presents its own challenges and opportunities; it can be exciting to consider working closely with someone you already know, like, and respect, and it is certain to change the nature of the friendship you had before you did business together.

When you decide to hire according to a person rather than a job description, you have the opportunity to co-create the resulting position together. You don't have to start with a blank slate; as the business owner, it's still your prerogative to set the tone and outline your vision for the position. Working from that outline, you can then collaborate to fine-tune the position to ensure that it makes the most of each person's strengths and meets your business's needs.

Be careful not to slip into being too casual about expectations and goals. It might be tempting, because you know each other, to say, "Oh, we'll figure that out," or "If it were anyone but you, I'd put numbers on these goals." You might co-create the description, but do it with the future in mind. There might be a time when the description will need to be applied to a new job candidate, and you want things spelled out appropriately. This will be particularly important when it comes time for performance reviews.

In any hiring process, it's important to take the other person's personality and energy into account and make sure they are compatible with your own. Notice that I said "compatible," not "identical."

You don't need to be the same in order to work well together. While two or more introverts working in the same space might sound like an ideal scenario, it might prove less so if you enable each other to isolate or avoid the spotlight. If no one in the office likes to pick up the phone or go networking, that's a problem! Ultimately, as the entrepreneur in charge, it's your job to make sure your company is out and about. Hire too many introverts, and you might find that you're all enabling each other to stay in your cozy cocoons.

The ideal solution is to hire someone whose energy complements rather than matches yours, whether or not that person is an introvert or extrovert. There are certainly "extroverted introverts" who enjoy the challenge of sales and networking (maybe you're one of them!). They see it as a task to be conquered and will approach it with determination and persistence. There are also extroverts whose sensibility makes them a perfect counterbalance to your introvert energy. They might have worked with introverts before or have close friends or loved ones who are introverts. You'll notice that while they have a more outward-turning energy, they are also good listeners and aware of themselves and the impact their energy has on others.

Here are a few other things to look for when considering a potential colleague:

- Shared vision—or at least shared understanding—about the direction of the business (most important for higher-level hires)
- Generally positive, can-do attitude
- Clear communication style
- Learning curve, both in terms of gaining knowledge about your company and about the specific tasks to be accomplished

Most important, pay close attention to how you respond to the person's energy. Are you are worn out, confused, or otherwise frustrated after being with him? If so, reflect on what was affecting you and consider if it was circumstantial or an undisputed part of his personality.

And finally, remember what's true for every human being on the planet: We are imperfect individuals. No one person is going to meet all of your desired traits. Nor is it reasonable to expect anyone else to be as passionate and committed to your business as you are. It's possible that you will find the "ideal" candidate. But chances are you'll find yourself weighing pros and cons and thinking, "Yeah, she'll be good in this role." Just make sure the pros outweigh the cons. Your business is too important to settle.

Why Growth Requires Paying Attention to the Forest and to the Trees

Remember the expression about not seeing the forest for the trees? This little phrase sums up precisely the dangers that await the entrepreneur about to embark on a period of growth. The trees— they're everywhere! And the forest—the big picture—well, it's in there . . . somewhere . . .

This can be an especially true situation for the introvert entrepreneur. Our inward orientation sometimes leads us to focus in on details and all of the little moving parts. Attention to detail is absolutely critical. You must be able to see and identify each of the trees that surround you. But don't overlook the forest. The forest is your *why*. It's why you're in business in the first place. It's your purpose, vision, and core.

Let's consider an example: One of my clients, who works within a larger organization but has an entrepreneurial role, determined that her *why* was, "I make good things happen." Sounds pretty simple, doesn't it? But it's that simplicity and clarity that gives her an anchor when the *whats* and *hows* are swirling around her. She can look at the trees through that lens and use a basic question—How does this create something good?—to guide her actions.

It's easy to become fixated on the *what* of your business. In the case of my client, if she is too focused on implementation, she risks losing track of the *why*, which is about positive results, not specific products or services.

As your business grows, it's critical that you keep the forest front and center in your thoughts, even when the trees threaten to crowd it out. The *why* of your business helps you make the big decisions, including what direction to grow in and who to bring on board.

It also has another benefit: It helps you keep a lighter hold on the reigns. If the most important thing is to make good things happen, then you have to be open to the idea that there are multiple ways to achieve that if you want to be successful. The *how* or *what* of the matter isn't quite as important as the ultimate goal.

I am constantly circling back to a phrase I've mentioned before: "I am open to outcome, not attached." These words, shared with me by a coaching colleague, have been a tremendous gift to me as I expand and try new things. I've noticed—in myself and in my clients—that when we're struggling, when we're feeling frustrated because something's not going the way we want it to, or someone's not acting in the way we expect her to act, our stress is caused by one fundamental reason: attachment.

If you're attached, you're clinging as if to a life raft to a particular outcome. As soon as you're attached, you become *too* focused and therefore inflexible. You can't adjust to the unforeseen because only a certain path is acceptable.

A more desirable state of mind is one that allows you to release expectations, "should" thoughts, and assumptions and stops you from going down the rabbit hole of "What if?" From that space of unattachment, you're better equipped to ride over, or even smooth out, any bumps in the road.

Is any of this easy? No. This is a good time to repeat a quote from Chapter 2: "The pathway is smooth. Why do you throw rocks before you?" So often, we create our own obstacles. Those rocks frequently show up as attachment to a person, place, idea, or outcome. They can be hard to spot because they are often disguised as goals. But what if it's necessary to change the goal? What happens if we're too attached to that specific outcome? And what if we need to course-correct because where we are headed is no longer on the map?

We are more likely to arrive at our destination successfully, all in one piece, if we are open to where the journey takes us rather than forcing a particular outcome. It can be uncomfortable, and we might resist letting go of the rocks (after all, those rocks often think they're keeping us safe because they allow us to hide behind excuses). But once we recognize how many rocks we are throwing in front of us—or how we turn existing pebbles into boulders—we can start to shift our presence into being more open and curious, less fearful and closed. And that makes the potentially overwhelming business of growth a lot more enjoyable for all concerned.

There's one more additional benefit to being open to outcome, not attached. When you release the need to control everything, you will be more open to influence from other people. You'll be a better listener and more thoughtful about ideas that come your way. And you're less likely to be in a competitive mindset with people in your industry. Why? Because you're a sponge, soaking things up, bouncing back, and twisting and flexing with the situation, instead of a cinder block, crumbling apart when someone takes a hammer to it. You'll take things in, use what works and helps you manifest your *why*, and wring out the rest.

Introvert Entrepreneur Focus

Jadah Sellner, cofounder of Simple Green
Smoothies and jadahsellner.com

You proclaim "I'm an introvert" in the heart of your business bio. What's important to you about putting that out there?

I make a point to share that I'm an introvert to show that even if you guard your energy, space, and time with how you relate to the world and the people in it, it is still completely possible to build a thriving online business with raving fans, which I have been able to do with Simple Green Smoothies. In just two short years, Simple Green Smoothies connects with over one million fans through our email and social media accounts.

One of my strengths is being a relator. And I find this to be true for many people who steer closer on the introvert side of the spectrum. We crave deeper, more intimate relationships with a small group of people. When I'm at large conferences, surrounded by big groups of people, I freeze and feel really uncomfortable. I find myself disappearing often to recharge and conserve my energy. But I use this to my advantage by looking for one person that I'd like to connect with for the day. And then they become my new best friend. They feel seen and heard.

As your community and business expands, what intentional choices have you made that help you honor your introvert energy and core values?

It's taken me a while to embrace my introvert energy and core values. I always thought people must think I'm stuck up because I'm so quiet in large groups. As my community and business expands, here are some things I've put in place.

1. **Build a team of extroverts.** A great tip I got from one of my good friends and mentor, Jonathan Fields, is to surround yourself with raging extroverts. My business partner, Jen Hansard, is an extrovert, so when we go to conferences together, she leads the way and dives into conversations head first. Our Community Happiness Specialist is an extrovert, and she just lights up getting to stay in conversations with our community all day long.

2. **Give permission to recharge.** Over the years, I've learned to not be so judgmental with myself when I start to feel overwhelmed by people and their energy. If I slip away from a conversation or a luncheon, I give myself permission to retreat into a quiet place, or my hotel room, and I tell myself that's OK. It allows me to fully show up later in the day. I just say, "I need to rest for a little bit, I'll see you later."

3. **Schedule connection time.** Being in deep relationships is important to me. But because it's so easy for me to stay indoors, in my pajamas, and behind my laptop or a book all day, I have to make sure I schedule time with the people I care most about. I make sure to schedule lunch and dinner dates with my husband and daughter, so I don't miss out on connection time. I also make bookend dates with friends and family to give my mind and body a break from my work.

I feel safe when I'm alone, but I know my core value is to connect with my close circle of friends and family. So the first important thing to know is who falls into that circle. And then they are always a *yes*. Once you've identified who is a part of your safety circle, it's easier to guard your time and energy and say no to anyone outside of that circle.

With growth comes increased demands on our time and energy—more people want a piece of us! What's your advice for an introvert entrepreneur navigating the relationship-building aspect of a growing business?

As my business grows, I have to create an ongoing practice of checking back in with what's most important to me. I plan my year by quarters with my business partner, and I review my goals and dreams with my husband every year. This allows the people most important to me in my business and personal life to be on the same page with me. As more opportunities and shiny objects come my way, being clear on what's most important for that year makes it easier to say no. It's not easy, just easier. I've also become a fan of sending quick responses to invitations that I must decline with lots of love. Here's an example of a recent email I sent:

"I'm actually going to be in super hustle mode for January through March for writing and creating new recipes for our Simple Green Smoothies book. I've already planned out the weekends where I'll play, rest, recharge. So I have to jump on the 'no' train for everything else."

Chapter 9

Accelerating Failure, Staying in Your Comfort Zone, and Other Ways to Set Yourself Up for Success

You Miss Every Shot You Don't Take

Consider this question: How long does it take to build a business or do anything at which you want to be successful?

It depends on how many shots you're willing to take.

Imagine you're at the county fair, and you've decided you want to win a stuffed animal for your three-year-old son. Your options include five chances to toss a ring onto a post or ten attempts to whack a mole back down into a hole. Why do they give you so many opportunities, when you just need to succeed once?

In the context of the fair, we have a clear understanding of what's going on. We know that we need several tries before we succeed because the game is set up to be challenging (but we hope not unwinnable). Out of five tosses, we might get the ring on the post once . . . and chances are it will be one of our last attempts.

We've learned to assume we won't win the stuffed animal on

the first try. We need multiple opportunities, practice tosses, and commitment to stick with it, even if we feel frustrated.

So why do we forget all of that when it comes to our business development?

Putting the Odds in Your Favor

Fall seven times, stand up eight.   —Japanese proverb

My business development action plan includes some activities that are well within familiar territory, and in some ways much easier than whack-a-mole: Write blog posts and articles. Produce podcasts. Coach clients.

It also includes stuff that feels vulnerable to this introvert: Deliver presentations. Go to networking events. Email and call people I don't know.

I have to do these activities consistently and frequently so that of the five times I present the same information, there will be one time that results in a solid business lead. If I want the odds to be in my favor, I must do the uncomfortable tasks alongside the comfortable ones, over and over and over again.

Just the idea of it pushes the buttons inside me labeled "insecure!" and "Who are *you* to think you can . . . ?" We can feel exposed as we keep putting ourselves out there, making the internal external. This is especially true if we think that every attempt has to be perfect. When we start going down the path of insecurity and doubt, it's easy to turn inward and think that we can figure it out all by ourselves. Then we remember how important it is to shine the light on the fears so that they don't fester in the dark recesses of our brain.

You've probably heard the expression, "What we resist, persists." The fear will keep knocking until you open the door. The turning point comes when you can see the fear for what it is, deal with it, and get on with the job. You can't let the resistance keep you from taking imperfect action. As Wayne Gretzky said: "You miss 100 percent of the shots you don't take."

So if you don't email, if you don't pick up the phone, then 100 percent of those people won't learn about how you can help them. They won't have the opportunity to say "Tell me more." Instead, you're saying no preemptively, on their behalf.

And why the heck would you want to do that? Why would you make that decision for them?

There are times when we can get too much in our head, choosing to retreat into our introversion rather than channel it. Or we'll start making excuses and deciding it's more important to go match up all of our socks. When that happens, remind yourself why you do what you do and the responsibility you have to bring your particular gifts out into the world.

The tension introvert entrepreneurs often experience stems from what they feel called to do and what's required of them to do it. By its very nature, being of service to other people means we're going to work and interact with people in some capacity. There are definitely times when we're not going to feel up to the task. In those cases, ask yourself these centering questions: Why did I start my business? What problem am I solving for people? To what, and to whom, do I feel responsible? Use your answers to remind yourself of why it's important that you keep showing up and offering your work to the people who are counting on you. Consider if the people you counted on stopped doing what they do; wouldn't your life be a bit poorer because of it? The people you serve feel the same way about you.

The bottom line is really quite simple: All you have to do is show up authentically, trust in and share your value, make an offer, and see what happens. You need to be curious and understand that each failure brings you one step closer to the success you seek. When you allow curiosity to replace fear, failure can become your friend.

Improv and the Introvert: An Unlikely Combination

In that spirit and as I've mentioned previously, it's valuable to learn how to accelerate—and embrace—failure.

That's where improvisational theater techniques have helped me the most because improv is all about making lemonade when you're handed a lemon.

For me, improv pushes every button in my book. That's why one of the first emails I sent after I started the Introvert Entrepreneur was to a colleague who conducted improv classes: The idea of actually learning to do improv excited and scared me, and I sensed that it would be a powerful experience. I'd had some exposure to it in an earlier workshop. That time, I hesitated to jump into anything that was more than making a sound or tossing an object. It was too much to be put on the spot in front of a group of strangers. As an introvert, I like to be prepared and know what's going to happen next, what's expected of me. I don't like being caught off guard. Once we moved past the warm-up activities and got into exercises that required actual words, the fear set in. I fell into the bad habit of listening while simultaneously trying to figure out what I was going to say when it was my turn. That meant I wasn't really listening at all. When suddenly it was my turn, I'd stutter and blurt out something that made no sense, at least to my ears. Improv is excruciating, from that perspective.

However, as I found over the course of the numerous workshops I hosted with colleagues, improv is also fun. It's liberating. It helps me trust myself, knowing that whatever comes flying out of my mouth is going to be accepted by the other person. This transformation didn't happen overnight. It took time to get used to the idea that I didn't have to dot every *i* and cross every *t* in my head before I spoke. Things happened quickly enough that I didn't have time to stop and wonder, "How stupid did that sound?" because we'd already moved on. And guess what? I survived.

The essential point for introvert entrepreneurs is that making mistakes and being willing to step into the unknown is not only OK, it's essential. Knowing this intellectually is one thing; trusting enough to do it is another. Trust may help you move forward but it doesn't cancel out the discomfort you feel at jumping into a situation with no set outcome, no guaranteed result.

Why Respecting Your Comfort Zone Is a Good Idea

In the world of personal development, the phrase *step outside your comfort zone* (usually preceded by the words *you have to*) shows up so much, I've decided never to use it again.

After all, why would I want to step outside my comfort zone? My comfort zone is filled with dark chocolate, naps, kitty cats, my BFFs, spending a quiet evening at home, and reading in my comfy chair. It's a cozy place where, according to those who want me to step out of it, I can turn into an indifferent blob of unchallenged humanity, complete with cobwebs and a layer of dust.

Telling me to step out of it is telling me to do something scary. I can imagine doing the scary thing, and just like stepping on a hot summer sidewalk with bare feet, I see myself bouncing back over to the cool, comforting grass at the first opportunity.

Because telling me to step out has always felt admonishing ("Get your rear in gear!"), I've taken to saying "*Expand* your comfort zone." Use each new experience to make the circle a little larger, to encompass more experiences. That's felt comfortable. Until recently.

What's changed? I have realized that the word *comfort* comes laden with judgment. Being in the comfort zone = bad/safe, being out = good/scary.

Now I look at my comfort zone as something I need and want. It's a safe place that recharges me. Maybe it's my introversion coming through loud and clear, but I think my comfort zone is just fine where it is, thank you very much.

Recognizing that there's still a need for an expression that indicates we're growing, I propose expanding our *capacity* zone. I want to expand what I'm capable of doing and being. By using the word *capacity*, I'm acknowledging that I have certain skills and gifts. It recognizes that I have inherent strengths. I may not be using them at full capacity, and that's where expansion comes in.

Words matter. Within this reframing, the context shifts: Instead of moving from bad/safe to good/scary, I'm moving from good to better. I'm moving from a place of power to expanded power rather than from weakness to relative power.

How Can Introvert Entrepreneurs Expand Their Capacity Zone?

Here are some ways you can expand that zone: Find ways to recharge yourself during large, noisy, and/or long events or when you're with people with faster/higher energy. *Learn to carry your serenity and safety around inside yourself.* It's OK to close your eyes for a minute . . . step outside for air . . . take your time in the restroom . . . wear earplugs. You can increase your capacity for staying in what may be a draining space by developing ways to quickly reconnect with your quieter source of energy.

And while you're at it, *stretch into asking for what you need or want.* When it's time to leave, leave. No excuses, no justifications. If you have something to say, say it. If you can't get a word in edgewise, share it after the conversation. Practice taking care of your needs as you go rather than letting others talk over or around you. When it comes to your energy and your needs, no one else is going to take care of you. You have to know—and ask for—what you want.

Make a choice to be *fully accepting of your introverted nature.* Author Sophia Dembling offers this personal insight: "Once I started thinking consciously about my introversion and working with it with intention, things that used to be very difficult became easier. For instance, once I decided I'm not obligated to answer the phone, it became easier to answer the phone because I do it as a choice instead of because I feel the world requires it. Once I know that I can leave a party when I'm ready to go, it makes it much easier to go to the party in the first place."

Make friends with the unknown. Introverts generally like to be prepared and know what to expect. Responding quickly, being put on the spot, dealing with unclear expectations—these are not high on our list of favorite things. Yet, as we know, life is full of situations and people for which we can never be prepared. In those moments, shift from fear to curiosity. Instead of thinking, "I don't know what's going to happen!" try thinking, "I wonder what will happen?" Trust that whatever happens, you can handle it.

If you need to build your inner trust, *take an improv workshop.* Improv is a safe, structured way to practice managing the unexpected and stretch your capacity zone. There are just enough rules to provide structure and shared expectations, and there is always permission to fail. Improv is about acceptance, authenticity, being present, and trust—all of which also give the introvert a way to create personal energy and safety in the midst of chaos.

While the phrase *step outside your comfort zone* might speak to some people, it doesn't speak to me. Perhaps you're motivated by the expression; that's why I always expect some pushback when I share my perspective. My challenge for you is to find a way to live in the both/and rather than in the either/or. You don't have to be enjoying comfort *or* being scared out of your wits. Honor your desire for comfort and you'll be more empowered to explore new territory. Start focusing on what you want to grow, building on what you already have, and adding new experiences that expand your capacity. And as long as you maintain ready access to dark chocolate or another one of your comfort zone goodies, you're going to be just fine.

The Sustainable Introvert Entrepreneur

> *I am in favor of [actions] that have authenticity, roots, originality, verve, balance, taste, communicativeness, challenge, relevance to their time—in short, things that make sense.*   —Václav Havel

Sometimes a word pops up over and over until we just can't ignore it. For me, there's been a recurring theme of *sustainability.* We most often hear about sustainability in the context of the environment or about the operations of a corporation or organization. My thinking was provoked during a coaches' association meeting a few years ago that featured a presentation titled "Sustainability: The Next Edge of Coaching." While it certainly raised some questions for me about my general profession, the more profound realization came when I asked myself, "Am I sustainable?"

Ask yourself that question: Am I sustainable?

There are two definitions of *sustain* that I like from the *American Heritage Dictionary*:

To supply with necessities or nourishment; provide for

To support the spirits, vitality, or resolution of; encourage

If you are sustainable, then you are taking care of yourself, providing for your needs, and maintaining a reasonable level of vitality and spirit. To borrow from the environmental context, it also means that you are meeting your current needs without depleting future resources.

When you begin to think, "I'm so tired . . . I'm burned out" and at the same time feel like you are working hard and need to be working harder, realize that you are making choices that are not sustainable.

Do you ever feel that way? Do you find yourself saying, "I can't keep going like this"? If so, you're sharing my pain. Let's look at a few of the choices that affect our personal sustainability:

Time. How well are you prioritizing and managing your time? Is your calendar full of shoulds and obligations that lead to regular exhaustion (mentally, physically, emotionally)?

Are you making adequate time for yourself, for friends, family, and even pets? If you had to have the same schedule you had this week for the next year, could you do it?

Money. Everyone's favorite topic, right? Just as we spend and save our time, how we spend and save our money is a reflection of our priorities. Are you living within, below, or beyond your means? Do you alternate between feast and famine? Are you able to cover the basics of today and tomorrow, while having the resources for small luxuries that feed your spirit, such as music, books, art, and travel?

Health. If you're not making choices that sustain your energy, you'll end up "running on empty." And just like a car that runs out of gas, you can become stalled and quit in the middle of the road if you are making short-term choices for short-term gain. Certain choices—fast food, empty calories, skimping on sleep, sporadic exercise—will sneak up on you in the form of extra weight, illness, or injury. Another pitfall is taking an all-or-nothing approach: no desserts, exercise every day, no fast food. Your intention and willpower may last for a few days, weeks, or even months . . . however, that approach is usually unsustainable. What choices will sustain your energy for the long run, while fitting into your lifestyle?

Alone time. This is particularly important for the introvert. Are you getting enough downtime to sustain your energy for your business? For other activities that feed your body, mind, and spirit? And are you able to carve out that alone time without guilt or defending the need for it? How do you acknowledge and celebrate your spirit? What nourishes you?

These are just a few of the areas to which you can apply the question of personal sustainability; others include commitments, relationships, energy, and work. Take the time to reflect on each area and ask, "Am I making choices that support sustaining a life that I love? If not, what options do I have to put myself on the path to sustainability?"

When thinking about sustainability, it's also useful to consider the concept of the triple bottom line. In the corporate arena, the triple bottom line is made of people, planet, and profits. The extent to which those are honored is the measure of success and effectiveness.

This raises another question for me: What's *my* triple bottom line? My immediate answer is ease, flow, and truth. If my choices invite more ease, flow, and truth into my life, then I am both successful and sustainable. How would you define *your* triple bottom line?

The Fine Art of Letting Go

Stay calm.
Don't panic
and
Don't quit!
Be prepared . . . if you have an escape plan and adapt to
the emergency, you greatly increase your chances of survival.
—Guest information book, Skamania Lodge, WA

As I read these words, they stand alone, perfectly. How to elaborate on them escapes me. And they are the perfect words to close out this part of our introvert entrepreneur journey together. They sum up exactly what we need to remember when change happens or when we need to let go of an attachment, a need, or the baggage that we've packed but never opened.

There's a difference between giving up and letting go. Learn which is which.

The advice offered by whoever wrote the Skamania Lodge guest information book brings forward many of the traits of successful introvert entrepreneurs: calm . . . focused . . . persistent . . . prepared . . . flexible . . . survivor.

If I were to add anything to its sage advice, it would be, "And keep breathing."

Ten Steps to Success as an Introvert Entrepreneur

1) Understand that building a sustainable business as an introvert is all about awareness, energy, and authenticity.

2) Explore your relationship to fear and risk, and develop strategies to increase your tolerance for both.

3) Clarify your values and what it means to show up as your true self.

4) Connect with others in ways that align with your natural strengths.

5) Activate your introvert superpowers to communicate your message and close the sale.

6) Nurture a community that becomes a partner in your business growth.

7) Establish productive collaborations that allow you to broaden your influence.

8) Expand your capacity and accelerate progress by entering into formal partnerships and employee relationships.

9) Honor your introvert core as your business evolves and demands more of your energy.

10) Commit to constant learning and skill building in service of personal and professional success.

Acknowledgments

No introvert is an island, as much as she might wish to be! This is never truer than when birthing a book. While the writing was primarily a solitary activity, what it took to get this book in your hands was definitely not. A warm introvert-style shout-out goes to the following:

Julie Fleming. It was in 2010 during one of your workshops that I realized I was being called to work with introvert entrepreneurs. One of the most memorable moments of my life!

Judy Dunn and Snowpocalypse 2012. You couldn't get on a plane, so five months later, I earned your unused Writer's Digest Conference ticket. And that changed everything.

Annie Bomke. You were the first agent I pitched at that conference, and you saw the diamond in the rough. I'm forever grateful for your wise counsel, enthusiasm, and unwavering belief in *The Introvert Entrepreneur.*

Marian Lizzi and Perigee Books. You recognized the awesome potential of this topic and took it on wholeheartedly. This book is more powerful because of your vision.

Christopher Flett. Opposite of me in almost every way, which makes you an ideal mentor. You talked me off the ledge more than once and pushed me over the edge when I needed it.

Arden Clise. My accountability partner extraordinaire. You were there for me through every joyful and tedious step of this process. Are you glad that "working on my manuscript" won't be on my priority list anymore? (At least until my next book . . .)

My Introvert Colleagues: Laurie Helgoe, Nancy Ancowitz, Sophia Dembling, Susan Cain, Jennifer Kahnweiler. You welcomed me into the conversation and inspired me to add my own voice.

More gratitude to those who contributed in ways large, small, and always meaningful: Laura Armer; Lynn Baldwin-Rhoades; Jan Berg; Julie Davidson-Goméz; Delilah De La Rosa; Mary Fossbender; Howard King; Kristen Lensch; Paul Messing; Susan Schmidt; Shari Storm; Lori Zue; every coaching client I've worked with, past and present; guests of "The Introvert Entrepreneur" podcast; and the fabulous online communities of Facebook and Twitter.

Most of all, my deepest gratitude goes out to my husband, Andy. You have supported, encouraged, and believed in me every step of the way. You're amazing, and I love you.

Online Resources

You may have reached the end of the book, but your learning doesn't have to end here. Our intention has always been that this book be part of a larger library of resources that bring you timely, relevant information that continually expands your knowledge and skillset. You can find these additional resources at TheIntrovertEntrepreneur.com.

There you'll find posts, articles, podcasts, worksheets, and parts of this book that landed on the cutting-room floor. There's also an opportunity to participate in an online, interactive program that mirrors each chapter in the book and provides more in-depth information and resources to support your business development.

Recommended Reading

The following is a list of selected books about introversion, personality types, and topics related to entrepreneurship.

You can find a more comprehensive list in the Resources section of TheIntrovertEntrepreneur.com.

Ancowitz, Nancy. *Self-Promotion for Introverts: The Quiet Guide to Getting Ahead.*

Baber, Anne, and Lynne Waymon. *Make Your Contacts Count: Networking Know-How for Business and Career Success.*

Cain, Susan. *Quiet: The Power of Introverts in a World That Can't Stop Talking.*

Dembling, Sophia. *The Introvert's Way: Living a Quiet Life in a Noisy World.*

Doerr, John E., and Mike Schultz. *Insight Selling: Surprising Research on What Sales Winners Do Differently.*

Gerber, Michael. *E-Myth Revisited: Why Most Small Businesses Don't Work and What to Do About It.*

Heath, Chip, and Dan Heath. *Made to Stick: Why Some Ideas Survive and Others Die.*

Helgoe, Laurie. *Introvert Power: Why Your Inner Life Is Your Hidden Strength.*

Jones-Kaminski, Sandy. *I'm at a Networking Event, Now What???*

Kahnweiler, Jennifer B. *Quiet Influence: The Introvert's Guide to Making a Difference.*

Kawasaki, Guy. *Enchantment: The Art of Changing Hearts, Minds, and Actions.*

Keirsey, David, and Marilyn Bates. *Please Understand Me: Character and Temperament Types.*

Okerlund, Nancy. *Introverts at Ease: An Insider's Guide to a Great Life on Your Terms.*

Olsen Laney, Marti. *The Introvert Advantage: How to Thrive in an Extrovert World.*

Petrilli, Lisa. *The Introvert's Guide to Success in Business and Leadership.*

Pink, Daniel H. *To Sell Is Human: The Surprising Truth About Moving Others.*

Sinek, Simon. *Start with Why: How Great Leaders Inspire Everyone to Take Action.*

Sobel, Andrew, and Jerald Panas. *Power Questions: Build Relationships, Win New Business, and Influence Others.*

Zack, Devora. *Networking for People Who Hate Networking: A Field Guide for Introverts, the Overwhelmed, and the Underconnected.*

Notes

1. Introversion 101

1 C. G. Jung, *Psychological Types*, trans. H. G. Baynes (London: Kegan Paul Trench Trubner, 1921).

2 Daryl Sharp, *C. G. Jung Lexicon: A Primer of Terms and Concepts* (Studies in Jungian Psychology by Jungian Analysts, Book 47) (Toronto: Inner City Books, 1990).

3 H. J. Eysenck, *The Biological Basis of Personality* (Springfield, IL: Thomas, 1967).

4 J. Bennington-Castro, "The Science of What Makes an Introvert and an Extrovert," io9, September 10, 2013, io9.com/the-science-behind-extroversion-and-introversion-1282059791.

5 David Keirsey and Marilyn Bates, *Please Understand Me: Character and Temperament Types* (Del Mar, CA: Prometheus Nemesis Book Co., 1984).

6 I. B. Myers, M. H. McCaulley, N. L. Quenk, and A. L. Hammer, *MBTI Manual: A Guide to the Development and Use of the Myers-Briggs Type Indicator*, 3rd ed. (Palo Alto, CA: Consulting Psychologists Press, 1998).

2. Fear, Doubt, and Other Icky Stuff

1 *Webster's New World Telecom Dictionary* copyright © 2010 by Wiley Publishing Inc., Indianapolis, IN. Used by arrangement with John Wiley & Sons Inc.

3. Finding Your Voice

1 William Deresiewicz, "Solitude and Leadership," *American Scholar* essays, March 1, 2010, theamericanscholar.org/solitude-and-leadership.

2 Tony Hsieh, *Delivering Happiness: A Path to Profits, Passion and Purpose* (New York: Business Plus, 2010).

3 Anahad O'Connor, "The Claim: A Fake Smile Can Be Bad for Your Health," *New York Times*, February 21, 2011.

5. "But I'm Not a Salesperson!"

1 Simon Sinek, *Simon Sinek: How Great Leaders Inspire Action,* TEDxPugetSound, video recorded September 2009, ted.com/talks/simon_sinek_how_great_leaders_inspire_action.

2 Adam Grant, "Rethinking the Extraverted Sales Ideal: The Ambivert Advantage," *Psychological Science* 24, no. 6 (2013): 1024–1030.

6. It Takes a Village

1 Scott Berkun, *Confessions of a Public Speaker* (Sebastopol, CA: O'Reilly Media, 2009).

Index

INDEX

About the Author

MIKE NAKAMURA PHOTOGRAPHY

Beth L. Buelow, ACC, was in elementary school when she outlined the marketing plan for her first entrepreneurial idea, twenty-three when she learned she was an introvert, and thirty-eight when, in 2010, she put the two together to create the Introvert Entrepreneur, a personal and professional development company.

Since founding the Introvert Entrepreneur, Beth has established herself as the go-to person for introvert entrepreneurs across the globe. She is known for her sharp observations on the introvert nature, her accessibility online and in person, and her willingness to reveal her own entrepreneurial challenges alongside intelligent, heart-centered strategies for overcoming them.

A professional speaker, certified coach, and corporate trainer, Beth has coached dozens of introverted clients, trained hundreds, and spoken to thousands, championing introvert strengths and establishing her expertise in entrepreneurship, communication, and leadership. Her coaching, writing, and speaking style draws on her experiences as a trained classical musician, arts administrator, nonprofit professional, and entrepreneur. She is an active member of the International Coach Federation (ICF) and the ICF–Washington State Chapter. Beth holds a bachelor's degree in music performance from the University of Louisville, a master's degree in music performance from Northwestern University, and a master's degree in arts administration from Indiana University–Bloomington.

Beth has enjoyed sharing her message that "Success Is an Inside Job!" with numerous organizations and corporations. Selected presentations have included Starbucks, Boeing, Bumbershoot Festival's "Words & Ideas" Series, Seattle University, PrimeGlobal, Xceed Credit Union, Ignite Seattle, MarketingProfs University, eWomen Networking, Northwest Human Resources Management Association Annual Conference, Northwest Entrepreneur Network, and *Puget Sound Business Journal*, among others. Beth has been quoted and contributed to blogs and articles in print and online for *Psychology Today*, *Entrepreneur*, *Success*, *Forbes*, *Fast Company*, *Inc.*, *Crain's Chicago Business*, *Aquarius Magazine*, *Seattle Times*, and ToiletPaperEntrepreneur.com, among others.

Her extremely popular podcast, "The Introvert Entrepreneur," features interviews with well-known and emerging introvert entrepreneurs. Since its launch in August 2010, the eighty-plus podcast episodes collectively have been downloaded more than 700,000 times.